JUDGE THE JURY

Experience the Power of Reading People

Alice Weiser and Jan Hargrave

KENDALL/HUNT PUBLISHING COMPANY

4050 Westmark Drive   Dubuque, Iowa 52002

Dedication

I dedicate this book to the memory of my beloved husband,
Harold Weiser,
whose love and support continues to sustain me in all of my endeavors.

Alice

To Olite and Ozite, who once held me in their arms and, I know,
still hold me in their hearts.

Jan

Contents

Chapter 3: What Makes You Tick?

Chapter 4: Let Your Fingers Do the "Talking"

Chapter 5: Don't Write Off Your Doodles

Chapter 9: Personality Typing and Birth Order: Everything You Never Wanted to Know About Yourself and Others, but Were Afraid to Ask

Chapter 10: Promise to Tell the Truth, the Whole Truth and Nothing but the Truth: Intelligence and Deception

Acknowledgments

The manuscript had gone for its first visit to the publisher, I took a deep breath and felt a wonderful sense of satisfaction. I realize, though, that this book carrying my name, Alice Weiser, and my co-author Jan Hargrave is really the product of many more people.

To start with, there is my immediate family. My sons and their wives, Larry and Annette, Chuck and Brenda, and David and Melanee, as well as my five blessings. . .Nick, Eric, Sean, Jamie and Samuel. They have offered their ideas and suggestions. I am grateful for their interest. I must include some others. If I did it alphabetically, there is Helen Ackerman, my treasured friend and confidant of many years, whom I can call any time of the day or night. Then there is Doris Boyer, my encourager; Joseph Cohen, who keeps me on the straight and narrow; Cecile Holmes, who initiated this endeavor some years ago; Michael Minns for his support and belief in my skills; and Dr. Judith Premazon, whom I know is smiling on me today.

Finally and what should be foremost, Jan. She came to me and offered to pool her talents with mine. Though many people had offered to join me in writing this book, it was Jan's knowledge, experience and animated persona that motivated me and gave me the confidence to finally write. **Judge the Jury** is an amalgamation of our area of expertise and together we have authored a treasury of knowledge. Now, you be the **Judge**!!

—Alice Weiser

ALICE

After meeting Alice and attending her seminar, I thought, "Body language-great!" "Subject matter-fascinating!" "We really could write a book together."

Since no one person can be an expert in all the fields of knowledge concerning body language; I have had the good fortune to write this book with a colleague who has a vast and diverse wealth of information and who generously shared her expertise with me. Alice's understanding of her field, her humanistic touch with the pen and her wisdom concerning the American jury system have made our collaboration truly a synergistic relationship.

Alice is a remarkable, dynamic, spirited, gracious and capable woman, whom I am delighted to call "friend." Fortunately, she chose to share a portion of her life with me; for that I am forever grateful.

—Jan Hargrave

Foreword

September 30, 1997

TO WHOM IT MAY CONCERN:

It is funny that handwriting analysis and body language interpreters are not as widely respected in our universities as are psychologists, sociologists and psychiatrists. Pity.

In the real world, court room trial, combat of truth and personalities, a handwriting analyst is far more effective and dominant. Trial lawyers have little time for untested theories. Life, freedom, estates are all at risk every day in courthouses. Of course the Federal Government has for years utilized questioned document examiners to compare signatures. I have found the art of examining human beings, their motives and life and health through handwriting analysts, when it is practiced by a true expert such, equally as accurate often more so, than the questioned document examiner. The psychiatrist can't even give you a rough guess opinion in the thirty minutes you get before the average trial to predict the behavior of twelve jurors. The sociologist may spend the entire time trying to figure out the social relevancy of the trial itself. The Queen in this escalating search for personalities is the handwriting analyst.

A close cousin is the person who reads body language. Again, the psychiatrists are skeptical. Possibly because many of them are wrong so often and slow even more often. You don't get three years of one to one therapy in a courtroom procedure. You need fast, accurate answers. While many of them question the validity of body analysis, none will be so bold as to refuse to admit that a mean glare or angry crossed arms means nothing. A tie clasp with handcuffs on it, the American Legion pin or a huge cross around the neck . . . these people are talking and no one can reasonably deny that. Of course you don't need an expert to figure some of these things out. The expert looks for signs the potential juror is trying to hide or is not aware he or she is making.

I have tried over a hundred jury cases from New York to California to Hawaii. I have used experts everywhere. The quintessential expert in the field is an attractive blond who used to teach dancing. She reads handwriting as though it were an autobiography of the subject; she interprets body language as though it were a sign language and the subject was intentionally speaking to her communicating his ideas and dark secrets. That woman is Alice Weiser.

Alice is simply the very best in the field. She selected the jury that awarded the largest counterclaim against a divorce lawyer in the history of the United States, in *Johnson vs. Daughter*. The verdict, in 1992 in a Houston, Texas court of $18,000,000 remains first.

She selected the jurors in the Brooks Hansen case, in Salt Lake City, Utah, where Mr. Hansen was unfairly accused of intentionally leaving $400,000 off of his tax returns three years in a row. The jury Alice selected found it was unintentional and Brooks not guilty on all three counts.

She assisted in the acquittal of the two Hobbs women in Boston who were accused of interfering with an IRS seizure. This story was the subject of a show on Geraldo in 1994.

If you have any questions regarding this fine woman's skills in jury selection, do not hesitate to call. I only ask that you contact her on the days that my clients do not need her in court.

Sincerely,

Michael Louis Minns, P.L.C.
Attorney at Law
THE MINNS BUILDING
9119 South Gessner, Suite One
Houston, Texas 77074

MLM:lh

The Writing's of the Court

Defense attorneys in Houston may want clients to improve their penmanship if an experiment by State District Judge Ted Poe proves useful. Well-known for his innovative probation techniques, Judge Poe has added a new wrinkle to pre-sentence investigations with the inclusion of a report from a handwriting analyst.

"It's just another tool like any other information in this report," says the judge. "Both sides agree. . .My hope is it will help in determining the defendant's attitude."

The judge met the analyst, Alice S. Weiser, when she served on a jury in his court. She joked about his writing on the notes he dispatched to that panel. Afterward she offered an analysis of his personality based on those notes and apparently impressed him enough to create the pre-sentence invitation.

Judge Poe says, "I won't comment on her analysis of me." But, Ms. Weiser did share one part of her analysis of Judge Poe: "From his notes to my jury, I could see he was a judge with an open mind toward new and different things."

Gary Taylor
The National Law Journal

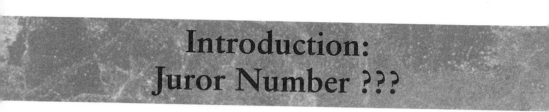

Introduction: Juror Number ???

Every effort was made to protect the identities of the 12 people who spent six weeks listening to the $10 million libel suit brought by a group of cattlemen against Oprah Winfrey. With juror numbers to identify them, these diverse men and women sat intently as prosecution and defense lawyers argued the case.

Partly anonymous until that cold day in February 1998, when a third-grade teacher, a retired farmwife, a mechanic; four males and eight females began deliberating the media-high, complex case that involved a superstar, a local cattle baron, free speech and the economics of beef. Before reaching a verdict the jurors asked U. S. District Judge Mary Lou Robinson to again let them watch a tape of the Oprah episode that sparked the trouble in April 1996.

Foreman, Christy Sams, a state employee, then delivered the jury's verdict: "Winfrey was not liable for any damages to the Texas cattle industry." Who were these people and how did they reach a unanimous agreement in spite of their immense diversity and different value systems?

TIMOTHY MCVEIGH CASE

The 12 men and women who spent weeks listening to arguments about the guilt or innocence of Timothy McVeigh said it was harder to conclude that he blew up the Oklahoma City federal building than it was to condemn him to die. They heard McVeigh's former friends talk about his anger toward the government. They listened with tears in their eyes as victims, survivors and family members recounted the horrors of that fateful day. And, they contemplated issues as defense lawyers presented witness after witness in an attempt to somehow explain McVeigh's actions.

After reaching a verdict and remaining anonymous until the end of the trial, the regional transportation district landscaper and single father, the Denver-area learning-disabled teacher, the retired Sears employee from New Jersey, the Vietnam veteran, the computer technician, the registered nurse and the six other members of the McVeigh jury appeared together on NBC-TV's *Dateline*. Asked what question they would most like to put to Timothy McVeigh, they said in unison: "Why?" This diverse group too, having never had the opportunity to ask one question, reached the same verdict.

O. J. SIMPSON CASE

Faced with potential jurors who had been exposed to the O. J. Simpson case, Judge Lance Ito focused on a single theme during jury selection: Could they judge the case on evidence alone?

On the first day of the key phase of jury selection—during the oral questioning known as *voir dire*—Judge Ito told the first of 84 prospects: "I am not looking for hermits . . . I would be very suspicious of a Rip Van Winkle that awoke yesterday and just learned of this case."

No one claimed total ignorance, but most said in their 79-page questionnaires that they could be fair and would be willing to look at the evidence alone. The first day crawled by, with just four jurors questioned by Ito and lawyers. The long route to finding 12 impartial jurors and eight alternates was just beginning.

Although Judge Ito, along with the attorneys, conducted the questioning of prospective jurors; prosecution consultants, handwriting analysts, body language specialists and defense advisors were the ones watching the jurors with an eagle eye. Exploring every emotion, evaluating facial expressions, observing nonverbal communication, analyzing writing and scanning clothing and posture, the jury consultant was there to WEED out those who would be particularly negative to the case.

Lawyers spend a good part of their lives learning to communicate technical issues verbally. Yet research proves that jurors focus on nonverbal communication for more than 90 percent of the message. Studies have proven that people retain only 10 percent of verbal communication.

Nonverbal experts help lawyers observe the emotions of the jury pool so they can select jury members capable of experiencing shared feelings. To sway a jury, lawyers must RELATE to them. They must enable a jury member to declare, "That's just the way I feel," or "That's just like what happened to my friend."

The time spent in *voir dire* is of the utmost importance to the success of the case. The best trial lawyers in America will tell you that, "any case is 85 percent won or lost after jury selection is completed." Why is it always over at this time?

How are the votes of jurors predetermined? By carefully studying and analyzing: juror characteristics, statistics and verdicts (**Chapter 2**); prospective jurors' handwriting (**Chapters 3 and 4**); their doodles and drawings (**Chapter 5**); their facial features (**Chapter 6**); their body language (**Chapters 7 and 8**); their personality and birth order (**Chapter 9**); and their general intelligence (**Chapter 10**).

These nonverbal clues can tell you the juror's:

◆ approach to problem solving,

◆ treatment of others,

◆ emotional level,

◆ manner of dealing with conflict,

◆ social style,

◆ organizational tendencies,

◆ preferred method of reaching conclusions,

◆ attitude,

◆ sincerity,

◆ intellectual capability, and

◆ degree of sympathy towards others.

Carefully prepared and creatively conducted jury screening can lead to successful results in almost every court case. Just as the information contained in this book can help in the courtroom, knowledge of these facts are just as helpful in an individual's personal life.

Judge The Jury: Experience The Power Of Reading People will teach you how to listen and what to look for in yourself and those around you, so you can identify underlying motives, expectations and fears.

Learn to listen with a different ear—the one that hears what isn't being said. Learn to see with a different eye—the one that watches what's not being spoken. This book will start you thinking, seeing, listening and feeling about your life and your relationships differently and may give you the perspective you need to change them.

Learn how to "read" people, predict their behavior and understand how they're "reading" you. The clues that reveal the truth about those around you could help you to make better and more intelligent life choices.

A PERSONAL NOTE . . . ALICE AND JAN

While collaborating on this book we simultaneously nudged each other and said, "Could you picture HER on a jury for sexual harassment?"

We realized at that juncture that we were both viewing the world as if it were a jury assembly room and envisioning everyone as a potential juror. We observed the way they carried themselves, their attire, their interaction with others, their overall body language, their jewelry, their reading material, in fact, their entire demeanor. Then, we decided on what type of case they might best relate.

People reading continues to fascinate both of us and we have much to teach. Join us in this enlightening journey into yourselves and others.

Judge the Jury

You can't do anything about the length of your life, but you can do something about its width and depth.

A fundamental right in the American system of justice is the right to a trial by jury. Every year over 300,000 people in America take an oath and promise that they will decide with fairness the fate of another person.

The World Book Encyclopedia defines a jury as "a group of persons selected to hear evidence in a court of law and sworn to give a decision in accordance with the evidence presented to them." The United States acquired the Jury System from England. The fact that there are 12 jurors dates back to Biblical times. . .the 12 Tribes of Israel. . .the 12 Disciples of Christ. It has even been suggested that the 12 months of the Zodiac were taken into consideration, further fostering impartiality, in order that there be equal representation on the panel.

A question often asked is, "What do you call 12 people who decide which of two attorneys is better?" The answer: a jury.

Any time the facts of a civil or criminal case are in dispute, the parties have a right to have their case heard by a jury who will make decisions without bias or prejudice. Receiving a jury summons and serving on a jury is an honor and places an individual in the center of the most basic right of all Americans.

A Day in the Life of a Juror

Each trial is as unique as the people involved and its duration is unpredictable. A trial can last a day, two weeks or three months. On the very first day and all through the trial the judge tells the jurors what time they need to be in court each day and at what time to expect the day to end.

Trials Follow a Set Procedure

Jury selection: After the jury summons is received, a prospective juror reports at his specified time to the jury assembly room and is generally assigned to a specific case. He is then escorted to a designated courtroom and at this point the jury consultant assists the attorney in the jury selection process.

Jury selection is the term most often used, however, it is basically incorrect. A more appropriate term would be jury "un-selection." It is not a matter of stacking the jury, as no one has ever decided who will be seated in the jury box; but rather, who will not be seated in the jury box, or who would be the deterring juror or the person most negative to the case.

Jury consultant: An individual trained to analyze human reaction of feeling or attitude that is expressed in a body-language channel, i.e., facial expression, posture, vocal intonation, eye movement, lines in the face, type of smile or handwriting.

Voir dire: Voir dire (to tell the truth) refers to the advanced questioning of a potential juror or witness to determine objectivity and truthfulness before he is allowed to become an official participant in the due process of the case.

Venireman: A person summoned to serve on a jury by a writ or venire.

Opening statements: The judge or the attorney for each side explains the case, outlines any evidence that will be presented and discusses the issues to be decided. The opening statement is usually broad and sets the stage for the witnesses and details to follow.

Presentation of evidence: Testimony of witnesses and exhibits are considered to be evidence. Any exhibits brought out during the trial will also be available to the jury during their deliberations. It is imperative that jurors pay careful attention to the presentation of evidence since they will be deciding the case on the facts presented.

Rulings by the judge: The judge may be asked to decide questions of law during the trial. He may, at specific times during the trial, ask jurors to leave the courtroom while lawyers present legal arguments.

Instructions to the jury: After all evidence has been presented, the judge may give the jury the Charge of the Court. This includes legal instructions about the case and the questions the jury must answer.

Closing arguments: This time is given to the lawyers as an opportunity to summarize the evidence and to try to persuade the jury to accept their client's view of the case.

Jury deliberations and decisions: After hearing the closing arguments, the jury is sent to deliberate. During deliberations, members of the jury will decide how they will answer the questions presented in the Charge of the Court, then return a verdict.

The sequestered jury: Sequestration, by its very definition means to keep something or someone apart from all others; to isolate; occurs when the court does not want jury members influenced by outside forces.

JURY UN-SELECTION

Most successful trial attorneys in the country agree that 85 percent of cases are won or lost the instant that jury selection is completed. Jury selection **IS** the most important phase of the trial; research on jury dynamics has consistently indicated that most jurors decide guilt or innocence by the conclusion of the opening statement and some in the first 45 seconds after being seated. Factors such as appearance, prior publicity or preconceived ideas have an enormous impact on a possible juror's opinion of a case and should never be underestimated. Creatively conducted jury screening can lead to positive results in the majority of court cases.

Attorneys are successfully trained on how to communicate technical issues, and do so for the majority of the trial. Yet studies show that when jurors listen to evidence, they gather 55% of their information from the speaker's body language, 38% from his voice inflection and only 7% from the words spoken. Knowing this, valuable information can be obtained about prospective jurors from careful observation of their body language. Jurors enter the courtroom with preconceived prejudices, feelings, passions, biases and beliefs that serve as obstacles in information gathering. When a person tries to hide his feelings, speech is carefully monitored and the rest of the body is ignored. Since this is true and since the courtroom is intimidating, careful observation of mixed messages from jurors can give valuable clues to their intended communication. This strained atmosphere for questioning inhibits truthful answers and encourages socially desirable responses.

The more information counsel secures about a prospective juror, the better prepared counsel is to make effective and intelligent challenges in order to determine those best qualified to sit in judgment of another citizen or his cause of action.

Since the Supreme Court ruled in 1973 that one's attire, physical characteristics, body language, facial characteristics, or handwriting are constantly exposed to the public view, they are not within protection of the Fourth Amendment and can be analyzed during the questioning phase of jury screening. Today, more often than not, juries in civil and family litigation as well as in criminal defense cases are frequently screened or unpicked with the assistance of a jury consultant, handwriting analyst or a combination of both with much success.

Psychology and applied statistical techniques have a great deal to contribute to attorneys in jury selection. This inter-disciplinary approach can serve as an indispensable source of information for the trial team. The purpose of the analytical research, prior to jury selection, is to determine the characteristics of the person who, if not sympathetic to the client, is not antagonistic towards the client. Jury consultants, with their knowledge concerning human behavior, provide the attorney this scientific, thorough procedure for jury selection.

The research provided by the jury consultant is intended to assist the attorney in his decisions and should be viewed as an additional source of information to be evaluated.

Before voir dire questions are asked, an attorney should carefully analyze the characteristics of the juror that would best suit his particular case. He can then construct a series of questions that can be used to identify which jurors most fit those characteristics.

Ideally, an attorney wishes to have a jury made up of 12 clones of his client. Since this is not possible, he seeks jurors who possess traits similar to those of his client. Stating that an attorney is looking for 12 unbiased citizens is truly a misconception; what he is actually looking for is 12 biased citizens who think as his client thinks.

If the attorney so desires and especially if there is sufficient funding, a demographic study can be pursued. To obtain an even greater likeness to his client and to further study characteristics of potential jurors, the trial team can also analyze the homes of prospective members. Upkeep of yards, bumper stickers on cars, burglar bars on windows and other exterior details of a person's home can help determine what type of person lives there. For example: Is the home surrounded by a large iron security fence, representing a crime conscious juror, or is the home well kept with a neatly trimmed lawn, representing a detailed individual?

An attorney desires a jury of one or two dominant persons whose thinking is biased toward his client and prefers the remainder of the members to be relatively passive in their views. Realistically, in jury selection, one tries to eliminate the jurors who are most dissimilar to the profile of the "ideal" juror. While deleting those jurors who would be undesirable to the case, the attorney must also keep in mind who he did not remove because that is his jury.

Attorneys are like professional golfers, in the sense that, who wins or loses can be the difference of one stroke. The statistical determination of the ideal juror profile, coupled with interpretation of nonverbal communication, the submission of open-ended questions by attorneys that are worded to elicit maximum information and data obtained from the juror's handwriting analysis can, similar to the successful golfer, be that difference of one stroke.

To Tell the Truth

The term *voir dire*, means "to tell the truth." This phrase refers to the advanced questioning of a potential juror to determine objectivity and truthfulness before he is allowed to become an official participant as a juror. This is the first part of the jury un-selection process. The truth, the whole truth, and nothing but the truth is used following a summons, when someone takes an oath to give required testimony, totally, to the best of his knowledge, about a particular situation.

Attorneys who ask open-ended questions to acquire information from a juror, obtain much more useful information than the attorney who asks questions of possible jury members that only require a "yes" or "no" answer. Careful analysis of the answers to open-ended questions, gives explicit information about an individual's attitudes, personality, predispositions and prejudices. Yet, mysteries pertaining to an individual's true character can only be obtained from observing his nonverbal messages. Some of the most brilliant moments a psychologist can have in analyzing a person occur while sitting quietly, paying little attention to what the client says, and letting his inner senses and intuitive skills discover what the juror is *not* saying. Nonverbal communication exhibited by prospective jurors, both inside and outside of the courtroom, and group dynamics should be observed. To gain the greatest insight into an individual's experiences of life and attitudes, the body language expert must note how the individual talks, his voice tone, at whom he looks and his choice of words. Scrutinizing prospective juror answers during voir dire allows the lawyer and the jury consultant to detect if the person being questioned is forceful, passive or somewhat defiant.

Another crucial part of jury selection requires the attorney to impart information to the jurors where he actually teaches them about the case and his client. In cases where the attorney is allowed to ask the questions, the judge will have the attorney make a brief summary or statement first, then proceed with the questions. During this time, questions are asked of the jury either by the judge or the attorney. Implied knowledge through statements made during this questioning phase contains information the judge and attorney want the jury to have and sets the tone for the continuation of the case.

A supplementary purpose of the question and answer period of jury screening is a time for the attorney to communicate his personality to possible jury members. It is a time for the attorney to condition jurors to his character and disposition. Since the attorney is in complete charge, acting and re-acting are very important. The attorney is the actor and director and the jury is his audience. Successful attorneys are those who are interesting to listen to, exciting to watch and who offer variety in their questioning. Rather than ask questions of each consecutive juror, questions should be addressed to the entire panel from time to time. Regardless of the intricacy of the case, complex thoughts must be said in a simple way and in a manner elementary enough for jury members to understand. Jurors have a tendency to trust people rather than lawyers, therefore, complicated jargon by attorneys reminds jurors of that belief.

RIGHT-BRAIN VS. LEFT-BRAIN QUESTIONS

Brain research has helped us understand why language ability is hopeless in the pursuit of subconscious, concealed or secret forces in the personality. The brain is made up of a left and a right hemisphere, each with very different functions. The left cerebral cortex is the language center (Broca's area) and is used when people communicate their conscious ideas to one another. The right brain, in contrast, has been found to be subjective, emotional and creative; it contains the deeper feelings of a person. Poetry, music, art, ballet and metaphors are powerful vehicles for conveying feeling because they are right-brain functions. Therefore, when an attorney directly asks factual questions of a prospective juror, the person being questioned searches his left hemisphere and accommodates the examiner by giving logical, reasonable and socially acceptable answers.

To accurately know and delve into the secret biases and prejudices of jurors, attorneys must ask questions that require answers from the right brain's intuitive, emotional side.

Lawyers practicing in states allowing attorneys to conduct voir dire have the opportunity to bring out the hidden feelings housed in the right brain in potential jurors. By employing suggestibility indicators, handwriting analysis, questioning down a correlated line, and nonverbal communication, which may not be obvious to opposing counsel, the attorney is able to discover buried secrets of possible jurors. Therefore, by reading subtle indicators of deep personality reactions and feelings that are normally hidden from view, a trial attorney becomes enlightened and informed without tipping his hand to the opposing council.

Each of us responds favorably to certain personalities because we relate to their tone of voice, demeanor, dress, style or looks. We trust them without being completely aware of the reaction or reason. If we are given a gentle suggestion by a person toward whom we feel positive and safe, we tend to follow the suggestion. When a friend and confidant proposes, "Let's have dinner together tonight," we automatically agree. However, when dealing with someone viewed as untrustworthy, we may find ourselves resisting their efforts to persuade us because their influence makes us feel uneasy. To identify jurors who naturally feel safe with him, an attorney can issue a soft command such as, "Good afternoon ladies and gentlemen, why don't you just sit back and relax while we have a conversation." Some will usually shift and recline in their chairs, thus indicating that they are unconsciously open to the attorney's ideas and influence. By suggesting that they sit back and relax, he is asking their right brain what he knows their left brain can't answer. This kind of nonverbal response is called *leakage*.

CROSS-CHECKING FINDINGS

Since we imitate only those we admire, like and respect, it is wise for the attorney to cross-check his findings. No single response is enough to reach a solid conclusion. Following the observation of the first subconscious movement made by the juror, it is wise to note other movements which confirm the findings. To solidify his belief in juror support, an attorney can try walking from side to side and see whose eyes follow.

Those who do not imitate the attorney have not made up their minds yet; they have not accepted the attorney at their deepest level of emotion and intuition. If the potential juror sits back and relaxes, cranes his neck to follow the attorney, and then cleans his glasses when the attorney does, that potential juror tends to already be emotionally biased in the attorney's favor.

The prospective juror may become aware that he is following or imitating, and inhibit his impulses. To reduce awareness of silent behavior, jurors should be distracted with thought questions. They should be made to use their left brain with standard questions with answers that are predictable, meaningless or insignificant. The attorney might ask, "How many here are married?" or, "Mr. Andrews, what are the ages of your children?" as he strolls back and forth. While tying up a person's mind with bland inquiries, a questioner can test the possible juror's unconscious resistance and feelings to his suggestions.

TESTS FOR SUGGESTIVE INFLUENCES

A broad repertoire of verbal and nonverbal suggestions can be developed for use throughout jury selection. Juror reactions to these suggestions can then be scored (+1, +2, +3, or +4) for a favorable disposition to the attorney. Tests for suggestive influence are of four types: directional signals, imitations, authority gestures and emotional expressions.

Directional signals ask those feeling positive toward an attorney to follow the attorney's directional influence when he strides back and forth or points to an object. Obedience to these directional signals most often means surface interest or mild liking and should be scored as +1. Imitations, which show willingness to copy, are scored +2 since they indicate feelings of association or likeness. Examples of these occur when the juror cleans his glasses after the attorney does or laughs when the attorney laughs; an insinuation of, "You're my leader; I'll do as you do." Authority gestures signify an even stronger inclination to the attorney's influence. When the attorney cups his ear, the venireman knows to speak up. If prospective jurors oblige, they should be scored a +3 because they are surrendering to the attorney's authority. Emotional expressions are given the greatest weight (+4), since their appearance suggests the arousal of deep feelings. When a juror rearranges himself in his chair once the attorney says, "Relax and make yourselves comfortable," it indicates that he feels safe and trusts the attorney. One would have a difficult time relaxing with someone he did not trust. Following is an abbreviated table of attorney suggestions and juror responses.

Although all of the numbers on the table above have a plus sign, negative responses or responses not viewed can be scored with a minus sign. If a venireman does not follow a suggestion, his reaction is considered neutral (0), but if he overtly displays resistance, the score is −1. All responses that are interpreted as indifferent or negative are scored −1 for simplicity, although they vary in degree of opposition.

The best method for using suggestibility is in conjunction with a voir dire specialist or jury consultant. The attorney issues the soft suggestions and

Attorney Suggestion	Veniremen Response	Score
Directional signals	*Surface responses*	
1. Walk side to side	1. Their eyes follow	+1
2. Gesture toward client	2. They look at client	+1
Imitations	*Shallow responses*	
3. Attorney smiles	3. Juror smiles back	+2
4. Attorney clears voice	4. Juror clears voice	+2
5. Attorney sniffs	5. Juror sniffs	+2
6. Attorney cleans glasses	6. Juror cleans glasses	+2
Authority gestures	*Deep responses*	
7. Attorney cups ear	7. Juror talks louder	+3
8. Lowers voice as he speaks	8. Juror lowers his voice	+3
9. Nods his head as juror speaks	9. Juror talks more	+3
Emotional expressions	*Profound responses*	
10. "Sit back and relax."	10. Jurors shift in their chairs	+4
11. "Do you agree with me. . .?"	11. Jurors nod or say "yes"	+4
12. "Imagine this scene. . ."	12. Jurors close their eyes	+4

the jury consultant scores the responses. The use of a separate scorer frees the main counsel to focus on his delivery.

Questioning down a correlated line is a method of questioning that reroutes the inquiry away from the direct line of examination that typically threatens people. It is a type of indirect questioning that reduces defensiveness and induces right-brain leakage of attitudes and values.

Main counsel carefully designs questions that appear casual and harmless to the untrained, yet can elicit extremely revealing answers to the trained and astute observer.

It begins with identifying the critical personality characteristic that will most affect the jury decision. Some prejudices and predispositions are generic in that they are generalized feelings toward a whole class, others are triggered by some unique quality of the case. Personality dimensions associated with criminal offenses that distinguish one person from another are: liberal vs. conservative; reckless vs. frugal; insecure vs. bold and daring; powerful vs. weak; hedonism vs. bland; careless vs. careful; devious vs. forthright; sadistic vs. masochistic; high regard vs. low regard.

Personality dimensions associated with personal injuries are: prodefense vs. proplaintiff; stinginess vs. generosity; dependent vs. independent; unaccountable vs. accountable; anti-gun control vs. pro-gun; internal vs. external; reckless vs. safety; patience vs. impatience; superstition vs. competence; uncommitted vs. committed; nature lover vs. nature hater; respect for authority vs. defiant to authority.

Once the attorney has established the traits most likely to enter the decision-making process in any case, an analysis should be made of all possible correlated traits which will provide the opportunity for indirect questions. In a personal injury case in which the plaintiff's attorney is trying to get an award that is proportionate with the client's injury, he realizes it is futile to ask if the juror can come in with a big award. Any direct reference to possible stinginess or extravagance, which is what the attorney really wants to know, is avoided and questioning proceeds down a correlated line. Questioning a possible juror about his actions following the discovery of a discrepancy of $3.00 in his checkbook, can provide an attorney with valuable information as to the juror's level of precision and meticulosity. Several questions down a correlated line usually provide enough information for an attorney to decide on that candidate. Having several correlated lines allows the attorney a fresh start of indirect questions as each potential juror is questioned.

Correlated lines of questioning provide a sophisticated method of indirect inquiry that aids an attorney in choosing a criminal defense or prosecution jury, a plaintiff's or defense's panel. A jury expert not only scores the answers to indirect questions, but also records pluses and minuses for suggestibility, handwriting traits (Chapter 3 and 4), nonverbal gestures (Chapters 7 and 8), and personality typing (Chapter 9). In this way, the final ranks allow the attorney to make practical, educated judgments about possible jurors.

While there is no substitute for the verbal skills of a good attorney articulating the facts of his case, choosing the right audience or deleting those who would be negative to the case, is of equal importance. Failure to give this part of the trial adequate attention to detail can lead to a disastrous verdict, even in a well-presented case.

THE JURY QUESTIONNAIRE

Typical questions used on a jury questionnaire or checklist in acquiring data on potential jurors follows. It should be noted that questions differ according to the type of case (murder, sexual harassment, domestic violence, wrongful job termination, personal injury, etc.) being tried.

1.   Is the juror in any way acquainted with any of the parties, witnesses, attorneys, etc. in the case?

2.   What is the juror's occupation?

3.   What is the juror's spouse's occupation?

4.   Is the juror male or female?

5.   What is the place of birth of the juror?

6.   What is the health and age of the juror? Useful information for long trial vs. short trial.

7.   Has the juror read or heard any information concerning the case through the media?

8.   Has the juror already formed an opinion?

9.   Has the juror served on a case before?

10.   Does the juror have any feelings about the type of lawsuit, the party's race, ethnic background, etc.?

11. Is the juror accustomed to thinking about damages?

12. Does the juror understand "burden of proof" or "beyond a reasonable doubt?"

13. Has the juror had any legal training or schooling?

14. Does the juror have any friends or relatives that have been involved in a case similar to the one being tried?

15. Is the juror a leader or a follower?

16. Has the juror ever studied medicine?

17. What is the highest grade that the juror has completed?

18. Has the juror ever been arrested or charged with a crime?

19. Does the juror have any hearing defects?

20. Does the juror have any physical infirmity?

21. What other occupations has the juror held during the past 10 years and what duties were performed by that juror on each job?

22. Where does the juror reside and does the juror own or rent his home?

23. Has the juror ever been an office holder for any state, etc.?

24. Has the juror ever been a law enforcement officer?

25. Has the juror ever been an employer?

26. Has the juror ever been discharged of jury service?

Juror questions for a *murder* trial might include:

1. Do you have strong feelings about guns? Please describe them.

2. What are your feelings about the death penalty?

2. What are your feelings about the death penalty?

3. In what types of cases/offenses do you feel the death penalty should be imposed?

4. In each state there are different levels of punishment for homicide; depending upon the circumstances of the homicide. Penalty range depends on the state; probation, imprisonment, or in some cases, death. Do you view life in prison without the possibility of parole as a severe penalty? Please explain.

Juror questions for a *sexual harassment* trial might include:

1. Do you have brothers or sisters? If so, how many are older and how many are younger than you?

2. What type of car do you drive?

3. Do you consider yourself a competitive person?

4. Are you a single parent? If so, how would you describe the life of a single parent?

5. What television programs do you watch on a regular basis and how many hours on a typical day do you watch television?

6. Do you watch "Inside Story" or "American Journal?"

7. When you read a newspaper, what section do you turn to first?

8. List your three favorite books.

9. Suppose your checkbook didn't balance after you reviewed your bank statement and the balance was off by $2.50. What would you do?

10. Have you ever had to deal with a "bully" at school, at work or in your neighborhood? What was that experience like for you?

11. Please answer the following questions true or false as they apply to you:

     A.   I can usually tell when a person is lying.

     B.   When I make up my mind, I seldom change it.

     C.   I always follow my beliefs.

     D.   I am often influenced by the opinions of others.

12.   Do you think sexual harassment is planned or spontaneous?

13.   Do you think that one's clothing or lack of it can cause sexual harassment?

14.   Do you think rape is an act of violence?

15.   Do you know anyone who was raped? How did that person deal with it?

Juror questions for a *domestic violence* trial might include:

1.   What are your feelings on the DNA test?

2.   Name three people you most admire?

3.   You have memberships in the following groups:

4.   Are you a single parent?

5.   Were you raised in a single-parent home?

6.   Do you have any hobbies? If you do, what are they?

7.   Did you like school? What were your favorite subjects?

8.   Have you ever been afraid of someone? How did you deal with these fears? Do you believe that different people react to fears differently?

9.   Do you think that reports of sexual harassment are under-reported because the victim fears retaliation, embarrassment or lack of believability?

10.   Have you ever served as a jury foreperson?

Juror questions for a *wrongful job termination* case might be:

1. Do you believe that being terminated from a job constitutes injury or damage?

2. If an employer discriminated against you on the basis of your age, would you be inclined to file a lawsuit against that employer?

3. Have you ever worked as a personnel manager or director or been employed in any personnel department?

4. Do you believe that supervisors are generally (always?) right in their decisions affecting those who work for them?

5. Have you ever disagreed with a superior at work?

6. Have you ever applied for a promotion for a position for which you were confident you qualified, but were passed over for someone else?

7. Have you ever been verbally harassed at work by a superior? Fellow employee?

8. Have you ever lost an employment position because that position had been eliminated?

9. Have you ever resigned from an employment position because you were dissatisfied with your superiors?

10. Have you ever been party to a lawsuit? Plaintiff? Defendant?

11. Do you believe that older persons, particularly those over 40, are treated unfairly in employment?

12. Do you believe that employees over the age of 40 are less efficient in comparison to younger employees?

13. Do you believe that the age of an employee affects his work?

14. Do you think people turn too readily to courts to resolve their problems?

15. Do you feel you are generally suspicious of people who sue?

Juror questions for a *personal injury* case might include:

1. Do you drive a car? Do you (or your spouse) own a car?

2. Is your car insured? With which company?

3. Have you ever been in an automobile accident? (Explain)

4. Were you injured? Was anyone else injured?

5. Has any member of your family, or a close friend, ever been in an automobile accident? If so, explain.

6. Are you a director of, or do you own stock in any insurance company?

7. Have you ever been arrested and charged with a crime?

8. Are you related to. . ., or close friends with any law enforcement officer?

CASE ASSESSMENT REPORTS

Careful, well-informed jury selection is critical in any case, therefore, case assessment reports are compiled at the completion of most trials. An example of a case assessment report on juror profiles for a tax evasion case follows:

Jurors with any of the following characteristics may consider the party on trial guilty of tax evasion:

◆ Read the financial section of the newspaper daily

◆ Invest directly in stocks and/or bonds

◆ Watch four or more hours of television per day

◆ Are not optimistic about their future

◆ Agree that the IRS is an efficient, well-run organization

◆ Do not agree that most business owners overstate their business expenses for tax purposes

◆ Report that their parents were strongly supportive of U. S. tax laws

◆ Believe they understand the concepts of tax avoidance and evasion, but do not understand them correctly

Also, the following characteristics were found predictive of a prosecution verdict:

◆ Female

◆ Part-time or retired employment status

◆ Graduate school degree

◆ Family income greater than $45,000

◆ Divorced, separated, or widowed marital status

◆ Independent political affiliation

◆ Rent a room, or live rent free with friends or relatives

◆ Carefully read every word of a contract before they sign

◆ Self, family, or close friend has been victim of a serious crime

◆ Self or close family member has not worked as a bookkeeper or accountant

◆ Self or close family member has not experienced severe financial difficulties

Characteristics found predictive of a not guilty verdict in this particular tax evasion case follow:

◆ Male

◆ Disabled

◆ Less than a high school education

◆ Family income under $25,000

◆ African American

◆ Strongly disagree that most people pay their fair share of taxes

◆ Strongly agree that most business owners overstate their expenses for tax purposes

◆ Strongly agree that small business owners are typically intelligent, hard working and honest

◆ Have investments in real estate

◆ Self or close family member has worked as an accountant or bookkeeper

Therefore, it is easily understood how "scientific" information collected and analyzed from various cases, venues, particulars and etc., can be enormously and accurately valuable in assessing a proposed jury panel.

THE POWER OF LIKING

Liking is a powerful force that regulates all human interactions and should not be overlooked. Just as important as eliminating bad jurors, is winning over good jurors. If the attorney is respectful and diplomatic during voir dire, some jurors will decide they like the attorney and will be willing to hear the case with an open and favorable mind. In *The American Jury*, Kalven and Zeisel reported that in one-quarter of cases, the jury acquitted the defendant where the judge would have convicted because of liking, sympathy, attractiveness and fondness toward the defense.

Three methods of producing liking in a short time are:

1. Liking is reciprocal. We like those who like us.

2. We like those who are similar to us. Since we trust what others say according to how similar they are to us in their values, opinions, attitudes, interests, and past experiences, a commonality of these traits brought out between the attorney and the jurors helps to win their trust.

3. Dress sharply. Research in interpersonal attraction shows that people are drawn to those who look well-groomed and tend to give heavier weighting to their ideas.

Michael J. Sakes, in his article on "Scientific Jury Selection" states that the only significant discriminator between jurors voting guilty and those voting not guilty was how they felt about the prosecutor. Those voting guilty, he found, liked the prosecutor more than those voting not guilty.

Juries relate to the official court family and observe reactions from the courtroom personnel and all persons in the courthouse area. It is most important for the lawyer to establish good rapport and a good relationship with the court family, and even the personnel in the coffee shop. If not, the adverse vibrations or lack of such a relationship, is sensed by the jury.

Trial counsel should consider everything about his demeanor, his appearance and even his car and how it will affect his relationship with the jury. For example, in certain types of cases, and in certain localities, the attorney should be cautious as to the type of car to drive to court. In one case, a juror was offended when one of the attorneys drove a Rolls Royce to the courthouse daily. In another, an attorney drove a foreign-made car and one juror became upset because he thought the attorney should be driving a U. S.-made car.

Since attorneys must think quickly and verbalize their thoughts at the same time, the job of evaluating and assimilating information should be handed over to assistants who can be used to help record data and observe the person responding to the questioning as well as the other panel members and the group dynamics. Ignoring the techniques and contributions from other disciplines (jury consultants) results in an injustice and a disservice to a client.

The voir dire should end professionally and powerfully. The ending does not necessarily have to be cleaver; it could be a loud, sincere "thank you," but a crisp ending is the appropriate and fitting sign of professionalism. Perhaps a speech containing the12 most persuasive words in the English language, according to Yale University, could be used. Those words are:

You

Money

Save

New

Results

Easy

Health

Safety

Love

Discover

Proven

Guarantee

Because each case that goes to trial has weaknesses, it is extremely important that the jury be told these delicate faults in the opening remarks. Being up front with the frailties of the case ensures that jurors are not surprised later. When an excessively perfect case is presented, it may appear to be phony.

A PERSONAL NOTE . . . ALICE

Can you imagine what I felt when I was assigned the seat in the courtroom along side an alleged criminal accused of bludgeoning to death a woman and her two children? Needless to say, I asked to see his handwriting before his chains were removed.

After studying his writing, I realized that he was a man with no conscious and absolutely no feelings of remorse concerning the crime he was accused of committing. The formation of the two letters, the *t* and the *f* in particular, indicated a distorted sense of values and a twisted philosophy. In spite of all this, I took my seat beside him, knowing he would not harm me.

In fact, before the case was over he was writing poetry to me, putting drawings of little hearts and flowers on it . . . now, that's scary!

The Consultant's Role in the Courtroom, Juror Characteristics, Statistics and Verdicts

Experience is the best teacher, but the tuition is very costly.

IT WAS AN ACCIDENT, REALLY!!

There's a rule of thumb about the speed at which an individual answers. It is most germane when you ask about intangibles—attitudes or beliefs—instead of facts. A well known restaurant chain uses a timed test response in their hiring process. They will ask the interviewee if he has any prejudices against other ethnic groups or if he feels uncomfortable working with or serving certain people. The longer it takes him to answer no, the lower his score. This question concerns a belief and requires internal processing. Someone who holds no such prejudice answers quickly. The prejudiced person takes longer to evaluate the question and formulate his answer to try to come up with the "right" answer. A laborious effort takes more time than merely giving an honest answer.

How many times have you been manipulated or taken advantage of by someone's lies? Honesty is at the cornerstone of every relationship, whether it's business or personal. Being aware of someone else's true intentions is undeniably valuable, often saving you time, money, energy and heartache. It is important for each of us to get at the true message beneath the words that we hear. In an ideal society there would be no need for lies, but we do live in a world of deception. Whether we want to play or not; we're in the game.

It takes at least two people for a lie to be effective—one to offer the lie and one to believe it. And, while we certainly can't stop people from trying to lie to us, we can keep them from being successful.

WHO ME?

Let's determine what you already know concerning winning in the courtroom. Answer true or false to the following questions. The correct responses are found throughout this chapter and listed at the end of the chapter.

1. An attorney wants 12 totally unbiased people on his jury.

2. Weaknesses in the case should be concealed from the prospective jurors for as long as possible.

3. A highly focused person with great concentration would find it hard to identify with awarding a large sum of money to the person in the wheelchair.

4. A woman may tend to be harder on another woman, especially if the other woman is more attractive.

5. Most jurors sympathize with doctors.

6. Usually most forepersons are taller than the other jurors.

7. Accident victims rarely reward more than they themselves have received in a settlement.

8. Thin people have a tendency to give lesser damage awards.

9. Bartenders have heard everything and generally can tell when they are being lied to.

10. The more attractive someone is the more likely he will be found guilty.

ONE, TWO, THREE STRIKES—YOU'RE OUT

Selecting a jury is never easy. There is no magic formula. Attorneys for either side have traditionally depended upon their keen intellect, their experiences, their expertise, and, to a large extent, their insight and intuition to select the right jury for any particular trial.

In recent years, however, many attorneys have given themselves an innovative option: rather than depending entirely upon their own skills and experience and always retaining complete control over actual jury selection, increasingly attorneys are calling on handwriting experts and body language consultants to assist them in weeding out potentially inappropriate jurors. By doing this, the attorney adds another dimension to the jury selection process.

Using sound knowledge and technique based on scientifically demonstrable correlations between handwriting, body language and character, the jury consultant examines whether a prospective juror is likely to be strongly opinionated, emotional, prejudiced or flexible. Graphoanalysts and body language experts can tell if a person is a good listener or confident or disinterested, and he can help pinpoint people who are capable of understanding and retaining detailed accounts of narratives, complicated medical testimony, or hard-to-follow governmental or business-related issues.

Jury consultants do not stack juries or even select jurors. They screen and point out personality traits, strengths and weaknesses of possible jurors through careful analysis of their handwriting, gestures, facial expressions and body language. They focus less attention on the ideal juror than on the person who could have a negative impact on the others. Consultants also try to choose jurors appropriate to the attorney's case.

Graphoanalysts rarely get the opportunity to see prospective jurors, but can work rapidly to come up with a quick and accurate personality description and decision through careful study of a individual's signature. Consultants who are able to see the panel utilize their skills in "reading" nonverbal communication and physical traits.

JUROR CHARACTERISTICS AND VERDICTS

Judge Alan E. Morrill, Thomas Sannito and Edward Burke directed and conducted a jury study in 1979 to ascertain characteristics and profiles of courtroom jury foremen, attorneys, witnesses, and jurors. Statistics were determined and documented as to their personal backgrounds, experiences and preferences.

The most prominent trait perceived by jurors in the 62 forepersons who were studied was verbal productivity. Seventy-nine percent saw the foreperson as either talkative, one of the most talkative, or the most talkative person compared with the others. Those questioned indicated that the foreperson was either the first, second or third person to speak at the start of the selection process.

In the study, it was noted that the leader who talked the most was not necessarily the one with the best vocabulary and that the warmer the individual, the greater probability of being elected foreperson.

Jury leaders tended to be the most confident group member or one of the most confident group members. Members of the study concluded that a person who exudes confidence would help them feel comfortable with their verdict.

Studies have shown that bishops are taller than priests, university presidents are taller than college presidents and insurance executives are taller than policy holders. It is not true, though, that forepersons are taller than other jurors. In fact, they may be shorter than average height.

The person jurors seemed to prefer was the talkative, exceptionally warm and confident individual. This person was also slightly above average in IQ, dominance and word usage and less than average in height. By initiating discussions, displaying cheerfulness and reducing their uncertainties with confidence, jurors feel this type of person takes some pressure off of them. People with towering size, dominant personalities and exceptionally high intelligence levels were viewed as controlling. Their presence seemed to overwhelm others to see things their way.

In addition to the psychological profile of the foreperson, demographic information was obtained from the study. Seven times out of ten, the foreperson will be a white man, age 47 with about two-and-one-half years of college, who is earning about $35,000. When the foreperson was a woman, her average age was 33. She averaged two years of college, had an income of about $30,000 and tended to be slightly liberal politically. Typical professions for the foreperson included professors, managers, supervisors, executives, foremen, administrators, etc.

The person who best approximates the profile above has the greatest chance of being selected foreperson. Using a simple checklist of these characteristics, the jury consultant can narrow the leader down to one or two persons. The greater the number of check marks, the more likely it is that this individual will serve as foreperson.

When the jury liked the victim, the defendant's chances of going free were substantially reduced; on the other hand, when the jurors strongly disliked the victim, they tended to acquit the defendant.

At times, jurors may reason that the defendant is too attractive or too handsome to be behind bars. They feel that he wouldn't have to turn to crime to get what he wants. If the defendant is grotesque, they feel that he will hurt somebody and that he should be off the streets. While dressing up a defendant will not overcome strong evidence, appearances may make a difference in close cases. When jurors were aesthetically impressed, they were more prone to acquit. The more their eyes were offended, the greater was their tendency to convict. Therefore, if a client is good looking and likable, the attorney's job will be easier, but if the client is offensive, with a harsh voice, the case may be in trouble.

JUROR OCCUPATIONS AND VERDICTS

One critical item of information to know about a prospective juror is his occupation. For each of 25 different occupations, tabulations were made of their independent feelings before deliberation and their final verdict. This analysis showed that secretaries, teachers and managers convict with alarming frequency. Occupations concerned with control and organization, concentrate on mistakes and may overact to deviancy.

Persons in jobs that demand precision, such as engineers, machinists, computer programmers, bankers and accountants often at first felt the defendants were guilty, but changed their minds after deliberations. Because they are in jobs of correctness and accuracy, these jurors feel some uncertainty in convicting a defendant after the typical disagreement produced by group discussion. They also demand more stringent levels of proof to be convinced.

The occupations which did not lean in either direction, toward guilty or not guilty, were nurses, factory workers, professors, clerks, social workers and truckers.

Women showed a slightly higher tendency to convict compared with men, but the difference was not statistically significant (respectively 60 percent, 53 percent). Minorities are slightly more inclined to acquit, and people from larger families slightly favored acquittal over those from smaller families.

Jurors who acquit the defendant are more likely to have no college degree and be married to a liberal, less intelligent spouse. Also, acquittal-bound jurors tend to prefer reading to watching television, have more children, be later-borns, have voted not guilty on a previous case, disbelieve that criminals are too protected by the courts, and do not agree that jurors too often acquit out of pure sympathy. The opposite profile is true for those who endorsed conviction.

An interesting combination of two items that becomes a strong predictor of initial verdict was whether the juror preferred a good book to television and whether the juror had ever been a victim of a violent crime or knew of a close friend or relative who had. When jurors experienced a violent crime and preferred television viewing to reading a book, they were more likely to convict. It seems that those who like to retreat into books and have never fallen victim to criminal violence are better able to intellectualize crimes rather than physically react. A summary of jury characteristics and representative verdicts follows.

1. People in management tend to relate to the corporation.

2. Athletic people can relate to the loss of a limb.

3. Thin people have a tendency to give lesser damage awards. Also true of people who have thin lips, thin hair and angular features.

4. Youthful people are more sympathetic toward drugs and draft evasion.

5. Teachers may tend to be negative jurors as they want to teach and persuade.

6. Engineers tend to analyze and are often narrow minded.

7. Bartenders have heard everything.

8. Artists are more tolerant than people such as farmers and bankers who are very frugal.

9. Deeper, heavier writers generally have strong opinions.

10. Few jurors sympathize with doctors.

11. Males like successful men.

12. People in the arts are more generous than bankers.

13. There are often harsh feelings between the affluent and the needy; they can sympathize, but not empathize.

14. Musicians, writers, and literary people tend to be generous and enjoy giving money away.

15. Women are often harder on criminals and on other women, especially if the other woman is more attractive.

16. Eye contact or lack of it, as opposed to a twinkle, is meaningful.

17. Beware of the person who is frowning over half glasses; they are often analytical and want everything proven.

18. Accident victims, who have sued and won, rarely reward more than they themselves have received.

19. Impatient jurors do not listen well.

20. Certain nationalities are warmer and more emotional that others.

21. If one lawyer is attractive, the opposing attorney is wary of certain jurors becoming infatuated.

22. A person well dressed for his/her station in life will tend to be liberal.

23. An overly neatly dressed person probably watches everything and will be frugal in making a judgment.

24.   Religion is significantly related to all the attitudes that concern a jury.

25.   Education and contact with metropolitan news media is linked with a liberal attitude.

26.   Low trust in government points to a liberal opinion.

WHERE DO YOU GET YOUR NEWS?

"Know thyself," said Socrates. This wisdom is inscribed over the entrance to the Temple of Apollo at Delphi and is also imprinted deep into the minds of each of us. This image serves as a basis or a foundation upon which our entire personality and behavior is built.

Each of us carries around with us a mental blueprint of ourselves that expresses itself to others in the way we carry out duties, handle others, and reach decisions. For that matter, the material we choose to read reveals a great deal about our level of responsibility, our degree of motivation, our untold wishes, and our concealed or secret attitudes and desires. Responsible people control their personal development as well as their career growth. Attributes that can readily be detected from the books, magazines or newspaper material they choose to spend their free time reading are important to observe.

People who begin reading a newspaper by starting with the:

Comics section:	are fun-loving, carefree and possess child-like qualities throughout adulthood.
Horoscope section:	are sometimes suspicious, skeptical and rely on others to make decisions for them.
Business section:	are excessively interested in finances and profits.
Lifestyle section:	are fashion conscious, want to be "with it," and are concerned with impressing others.

Front page:	want a quick summary of the news, are surface readers who rarely investigate the facts, are worriers and are heavily influenced by world affairs.
Puzzles section:	possess a competitive edge, are logical and has a deep desire to find solutions to problems.
Travel section:	are often risk takers and dislike being in the same locale for very long, or like to travel vicariously by simply reading about interesting destinations.
Obituary section:	are realistic worriers who might possibly be consumed with negativity or illness.
Sports section:	are highly competitive and considered winners by others. They usually possess a positive, unstoppable attitude.

Former Chief Justice Earl Warren stated, "When I pick up a newspaper, I always turn to the sports page first. It records people's accomplishments; the front page, nothing but man's failures." Those who read the entire newspaper from beginning to end are considered to be very thorough and well organized in all their endeavors.

THE PROSECUTION FACTOR

Jurors are far more likely to feel the defendant is guilty and vote to convict when they think or feel:

1. Society is too permissive toward sex.

2. Misfortunes are the result of laziness.

3. Alcoholics are moral degenerates.

4. Pure sympathy.

5. Courts protect criminals too much.

6. The death penalty should be used in some circumstances.

These items represent various facets of authoritarianism. These attitudes in jurors significantly dispose them toward conviction. The more a juror endorses jurisdiction or authoritarianism, the more likely is the juror to favor prosecution. The lower the score of these items, the greater are the chances for a vote for acquittal. The least favorable personality to have on a jury, one that is negative for either side, is the person who would "lie through his teeth" to get a place on the jury to see that justice prevails.

Besides the opportunity for deselecting unfavorable jurors, voir dire is also the time to conduct business with the jurors. It's the attorney's only time to indoctrinate and immunize them.

If the jury consultant and the attorney realize that there are several people who would be very biased to a specific case, the attorney is allowed to ask the judge for a reshuffle of panel members. Reshuffle, similar to that of rearranging a deck of cards, is when all the jurors names in a specific case are placed in a bowl and drawn again, producing an altered juror number for each panel member. This, however, is the judge's decision.

THE REASON WHY SOME OF US MAY NEVER BE SELECTED AS THE JURY FOREPERSON

Indoctrination and Foreperson Suggestions

The term *indoctrination* means to give jurors their courtroom identity, including certain beliefs, legal principles, concepts and opinions. Jury members usually don't know what their role is when they first walk into court. It is the court's responsibility to help jurors establish a courtroom identity or image which they can assume during their tenure for seeking the truth. If no one tells them what to be, they will probably be themselves, with all their prejudices, biases, slanted thinking and subjective values.

Jurors need to hold and follow certain doctrine, such as:

Presumption of innocence:	A juror will listen to all the evidence before deciding guilt or innocence.
Beyond a reasonable doubt:	The state must prove its case.
A preponderance of the evidence:	The scales have to be tipped only slightly for a verdict to be determined.

A defendant may not be presumed guilty, because he does not take the stand.

While judges and lawyers usually explain and define these argumentative principles to jurors, their effect often wears off shortly after the trial begins. Unless the juror internalizes the belief and makes it a part of his inner self, his prejudices and personal attitudes seep into his thinking.

The most common way to get the juror to internalize courtroom doctrine is to constantly call up words such as justice, duty, obligation, responsibility or equality. Words that make jurors smile with pride allow the attorney to create a sense of right and wrong in panel members.

APPEARANCE IN THE COURTROOM: CLOTHING AND COLOR IMPACT

First impressions are very important. Decisions are made about our economic level, education, trustworthiness, honesty, intentions, attitude and credibility during a first meeting. It's been said that, "We never get a second chance to make a good first impression." From the moment we enter a room, we create an impression on those around us. Our appearance affects the way others see us and it speaks volumes about the way we feel about ourselves. When we are dressed well and in a professional manner, we tend to display professional and proficient work habits.

John T. Molloy, author of "Dress For Success," states that what a person wears determines his ultimate success or failure in his business environment. Molloy advises that darker colors transmit authority, credibility and likability. Although dark colors are preferred in business, black should be avoided in the courtroom because it appears too powerful and has funeral overtones. Dark blue and gray suits build credibility. Solid colors and pinstripes are acceptable. Solid white, pastel shades and simple closely striped shirts are fitting. Ties should be darker in color than that of the suit.

In 1978, Molloy wrote "The Woman's Dress For Success Book," and indicated that a woman's best courtroom outfit is a skirted suit and blouse. Molloy believes the following with regards to a woman's attire, "A medium gray or medium blue suit with a white blouse expresses the most authority." Navy blue, charcoal gray and beige are acceptable suit colors, while white on white, gray, and pink are suitable colors for blouses.

Not only is the clothing of the attorney analyzed and important, so is that of the members of the jury. Garments worn by individuals on the jury panel are scrutinized for cleanliness, fit, appropriateness and style. Shoes are judged, fingernails are examined, and hair color and style are analyzed.

Color of clothing has a strong subconscious meaning and will stand out over the cut or quality of an outfit. Different colors represent different meanings, evoke different reactions from people and convey certain messages to others. Color adds excitement and helps one express himself. In general, lighter shades have been found to communicate a more approachable, non-threatening image, while darker colors communicate more authority and power. In evaluating colors, it is found that:

Neutrals: gray, black, beige, brown, navy, white

1. do not project a mood or idea
2. are impersonal, with gray implying, "keep your distance"
3. are good wardrobe extenders

Supportive colors: purple, violet, blue, turquoise

1. should only be worn when you are *not* the star of the show
2. are spiritual and regal
3. project a quiet mood and are very flattering
4. are considered cool, restrained and refined

Happy colors: yellow, orange, sunshine colors

1. are encouraging optimistic, inspiring to others
2. represent anti-gloom, and are charming
3. reflect amusement

Romantic colors: reds, pinks

1. express femininity or masculinity
2. are stimulating, personal
3. reflect an effervescent, lively personality

Exciting colors: greens, blue-greens

1. focus the attention on you
2. represent leadership and a superior personality
3. reveal impeccable, immaculate tendencies

The occasion determines the color to be worn. The darker the color, the more serious—more impact; the lighter the color, the less serious—less impact. Brighter colors project farther, therefore, have the most impact. Neutrals project least from a distance and have almost no impact.

Color speaks and an assortment of many colors together tells volumes. When presenting, wearing three colors is considered very ordinary, wearing two colors projects good taste, and wearing only one color is deemed as perfect. Color establishes a mood and sends a message of the individual's personality, character and disposition.

Eye arresters, such as scarves, rings, watches, tie clips, earrings, etc., should not exceed 14. If the number does exceed 14, the audience/jury feels somewhat distracted and is no longer listening to the message.

In observing clothing of jurors and of attorneys, it is found that clothing varies with the size of the subject's home town. The larger the city, the more important. The more money and social standing a person attains, the more importance is assigned to clothing and the more their judgments are likely to be influenced by clothing.

William Thourlby, author of "You Are What You Wear," states that there are 10 decisions people immediately make upon first impressions:

1. Economic level

2. Education level

3. Trustworthiness

4. Social position

5. Level of sophistication

6. Economic heritage

7. Social heritage

8. Educational heritage

9. Success potential

10. Moral character

Following is a typical jury screening report used by jury consultants/handwriting analysts.

Juror Screening Report

NAME: DATE:

Negative Factors

_____ Emotionally unstable	_____ Pessimistic
_____ Narrow-minded	_____ Intolerant
_____ Prejudiced	_____ Selfish
_____ Ultra-conservative (rigid)	

Hostilities

_____ Stubborn	_____ Willful
_____ Critical	_____ Aggressive
_____ Impatient	_____ Temper
_____ Resentful	_____ Domineering
_____ Argumentative	_____ Defiant

Low Self-Confidence

_____ Fear of failure	_____ Fear of rejection
_____ Self-conscious	_____ Feels inferior
_____ Weak willpower	_____ Vanity

Positive Factors

_____ Emotionally stable	
_____ Sympathetic	_____ Empathetic
_____ Generous	_____ Conservative
_____ High Ideals	_____ Sincere
_____ Patient	_____ Cooperative
_____ Optimistic	_____ Determined
_____ People oriented	_____ Sense of humor

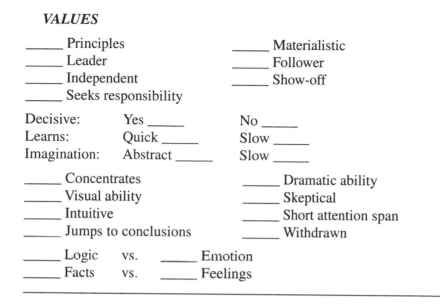

VALUES

_____ Principles   _____ Materialistic
_____ Leader   _____ Follower
_____ Independent   _____ Show-off
_____ Seeks responsibility

Decisive: Yes _____   No _____
Learns: Quick _____   Slow _____
Imagination: Abstract _____   Slow _____

_____ Concentrates   _____ Dramatic ability
_____ Visual ability   _____ Skeptical
_____ Intuitive   _____ Short attention span
_____ Jumps to conclusions   _____ Withdrawn

_____ Logic   vs.   _____ Emotion
_____ Facts   vs.   _____ Feelings

A PERSONAL NOTE . . . ALICE

On one occasion when I reported for jury duty, I completed the juror questionnaire and wrote my occupation as "handwriting analyst/jury consultant" on the appropriate line. Since I had travel plans beginning the following day, and was confident that my vocation would deter the attorney from selecting me to serve on this panel, I sat patiently in the courtroom. After much time and deliberation, to my amazement, I was accepted to serve as a juror. The day interestingly carried on as the panel and I conscientiously listened while both attorneys presented the facts and the evidence. At the close of the third day, once both sides had the opportunity to plead their case, we were asked to report the next morning to start deliberations.

The judge indicated that he wished he had sequestered the panel, but since he had not, he asked that we all be especially careful and that we report promptly at 8:30 a.m. the following day. His closing words of "don't anyone fall" made all of us feel somewhat silly, but completely aware that he was counting on us to make the final deliberations concerning the trial on the next day.

I returned to my home, quite exhausted from the emotional experience of the day, and had a quiet evening. I went to bed at the usual time, but kept the memories of the words spoken by the prosecution and the defense swirling through my mind.

I awoke the following morning and again began to think of the trial and the job that laid in front of me. Before I sat down to have my morning coffee, I decided to get the newspaper outside my front door. I had recently installed a modernistic alarm system for my home and as I exited my front door to pick up the newspaper, the new alarm blared loudly, frightening me and sent me flying across my terrazzo floor where I slipped and fell. I immediately called 911, the ambulance arrived and drove me to the nearest hospital. Once I was examined, it was found that I had broken my pelvis in three places.

The court was informed about my predicament, and felt that the information dispersed the previous days, by the court and the attorneys, was sufficiently detailed enough in order to finalize the trial with the previously selected jury members. To my amazement, the entire group was brought to my hospital room for deliberations. Braced in my hospital bed, yet still able to aid in discussions, after 5½ hours of deliberation, the other jury members and I found the defendant guilty.

This unusual case and bizarre deliberation predicament was a first for the State of Texas and delightedly served as my entry into working with the Judicial System.

ANSWERS TO "WHO ME?"

1. False

2. False

3. True

4. True

5. False

6. False

7. True

8.   True

9.   True

10.   False

What Makes You Tick?

A time to laugh,
a time to cry.
A time to grow,
a time to reap.
A time to live,
a time to die.

Each day blesses us with 24 hours. That's 1440 minutes. No more. No less. Time is relentless. It can not be replaced or reversed. Stopped. Stored. Or saved. Nor can we reach into our time reservoir to "borrow" an hour from yesterday to use today.

What is your "emotional clock?"

◆   Are you all "wound up?"

◆   Do you often feel "run down?"

◆   Are you "alarmed easily?"

◆   Do you frequently "run late?"

◆   Are you "slow and dependable?"

◆   Are you a "self-starter or a stem winder?"

◆   Do you occasionally feel "out of sorts?"

◆   Do you measure the "sands of time?"

The moment you place your pen on a piece of paper, you make your frozen mark in time and time is the essence of your life. The chance that anyone in the world could write like you is 1 followed by 27 zeros (1,000,000,000,000,000,000,000, 000,000). THAT'S HOW UNIQUE YOU ARE!

First Things First

Close your eyes and write your full name three times. After completing this exercise, what do you find? Your signatures are basically the same, aren't they? Handwriting is not a sighted fete. It is so closely tied to impulses from the brain that it is a barometer of our moods and of our physical, emotional and mental health. It might be called "brain" writing or "mind" writing.

Unlike one's fingerprints that never change, an individual's handwriting changes daily. Because mood plays an important part in one's nervous system, a person's writing is merely a portrait of himself at the time of the writing. Happy writing flows easily; whereas, writers who have just received unpleasant news tend to produce letters that have a tendency to tighten up and become more constricted. Mood swings definitely affect our script. When analyzing signatures for possible forgery, graphoanalysists note that the forged signature will never appear as relaxed as the signature that is written by the original writer when his eyes are closed.

Like facial expressions and body language, handwriting expresses personal characteristics. Watching a conversation from a distance, we can tell a great deal about the participants by noting their gestures and the looks on their faces. Likewise, we can observe the individualized gestures of handwriting as reflections of personality.

When a person picks up a pen or pencil to write, the brain sends messages to the hand and arm muscles and directs the marking on the paper. The lines, curves, loops and dots that result are all reflections of the inner self. Although the writing instrument is held by the hand, it is the brain that impels the writing to begin.

Handwriting evolves as the individual does, maturing with growth, disintegrating with age and changing; as a result of physical, mental or emotional illness. Although a person's writing can differ from day to day depending on his mood, physical health and environment; his basic personality indications remain constant.

Your handwriting is a portrait of you at the time of the writing. Think of the difference in your writing if you just found out you'd won the lottery and that of your writing if you were being audited by the IRS. Imagine being in the courtroom and having to write your name twelve times under oath to compare it to a questioned document. Would it flow easily? Would it be tense and tight?

Handwriting analysis is an effective method for screening prospective jurors, matching job applicants to certain professional positions and uniting intended lovers. Lawyers consult handwriting experts to aid them in understanding clients, jury members, key witnesses and opposing counsel and judges. It is also used to determine dishonesty as well as potential dangerousness. Document examiners use graphoanalysis training to evaluate forged signatures and spurious or altered contracts, and to compare one handwriting with another.

HISTORICAL DEVELOPMENT OF HANDWRITING ANALYSIS

Graphoanalysis is based on the premise that handwriting contains commonly repeated patterns which correspond to personality and character traits distributed throughout the population. The graphoanalyst does not reject the truth that we are all unique individuals, but as writer Michael J. Saks wrote in *Psychology Today*, "Our differences are vastly over-shadowed by our similarities."

Graphoanalysis can be defined in several ways, just as can psychology or intelligence. Perhaps the most comprehensive definition is the one that defines it as the study of the individual strokes of handwriting to determine the character and personality of the writer.

Psychologists use questionnaires, rating scales, and other methods of personality assessment in evaluating clients. Now an increasing number of them are learning the value of using an individual's handwriting as an additional appraisal instrument. Graphoanalysis is a *tool* that can be used successfully for assessment of personality traits and client disposition.

Formation of strokes, spacing of letters, slant and depth of the writing, reveal to the trained observer the counterfeit from the real. Graphoanalysis is a scientific method of personality assessment based on research conducted over a period of more than 75 years. This research, carried out by both empirical and clinical processes, is further validated by statistical studies, both within and without the framework of institutions of higher education.

M.N. Bunker, founder of the International Graphoanalysis Society, states "The accuracy of graphoanalysis is based on STROKES. The revealing factor is the strokes of the handwriting and not the letter formations. It does not matter what language the writing is in—even shorthand reveals the writer."

A person trained as a graphoanalyst can reconstruct the inclinations and the emotions of the writer of any adequate specimen of handwriting. The analyst can predict what the writer will do and how he will react under certain conditions. If a person were asked to write a paragraph containing his name and age and decided to subtract three or four years, the trained graphoanalyst should be able to look at this and see that there is a problem or an untruth. The writer is either nervous or is not telling the truth and the graphoanalyst will notice this difference by a slant change, an interrupted rhythm of the writing or possibly a pen lift.

SELF-ANALYSIS FROM YOUR HANDWRITING

Before embarking on our journey of handwriting analysis, write several paragraphs on unlined paper and place your signature on the bottom. Once you have completed your writing sample, look at all the dots, angles, loops, arcs, lines and margins; they reflect who you are, how you live and how you relate to the world around you. A person actually develops more than 600 variations from the writing method he was originally taught at the age of four or five and by his third grade teacher's penmanship poster. Through analysis of your handwriting or anyone else's, you will discover potentialites, character traits and emotional idiosyncrasies that you may have suspected or that you never knew existed. Because letters, strokes, spacing and intensity spark new awarenesses, you will never look at handwriting in the same way again. In fact, your friends may prefer to contact you by telephone rather than write a note because you may be able to discern the sincerity of their message and their emotional state at the time of the writing.

From one's handwriting a graphoanalyst can ascertain the person:

◆　　who has an attitude of superiority

◆　　who possesses a closed mind

◆　　who has a high level of concentration

◆　　who is restless

◆　　who feels a need for a high degree of authority

◆　　who is rigid

◆　　who displays a high level of gullibility

◆　　who is recklessly impatient

- who has a selfishness attitude
- who possesses certain sensitivities
- who maintains a high level of guilt
- who is broadminded
- who is generous and led by emotions
- who is extremely logical and judgmental

Because of the depth of information that can be gained relating to an individual's personality, prejudices, and character, it is readily understood why the art of graphoanalysis is so extensively used in the judicial system today. A graphoanalyst can advise an attorney about a potential juror who would either be beneficial or damaging to a particular case. The graphoanalyst cannot predict what will happen in the future, he can merely predict how one will handle emotionally what happens to him in his future.

In spite of its usefulness and accuracy, graphoanalysis has its limits.

- Handwriting does not reveal gender.
- Handwriting does not reveal age or physical characteristics.
- Handwriting does not reveal the future.
- Handwriting does not reveal handedness.

As you wrote your sample, you began each line at the left and continued writing to the right until you began a new line. Have you ever thought about what it means to write from left to right? Wonder no longer: the left side of the page represents the past, the self, or where you've been and where you are right now. It is the only margin in which we have total control; it is our beginning. The right side of the page symbolizes the future, the unknown and how adventurous you are. It makes sense, because the future is where you're headed when you begin each line.

Observe if your writing sample shows a rising handwriting, a straight handwriting or a falling handwriting. This imaginary line is called the baseline. The baseline is the imaginary line on which we write. We usually start to write by positioning the pen or pencil on this line, and then move away from this point in creating a handwriting stroke (normally in an upward direction), followed by a stroke downward to complete the letter.

By doing so, we have established a base for the letter and those that follow. The baseline is the foundation upon which every thing is built.

The baseline is not arbitrary but comes from your very nature and as such is one of the most important of all handwriting indicators. In fact, it is a strong indicator of the foundation on which your personality stands. It represents your sense of reality, your relationship to the here and now and your way of integrating emotion into daily life.

The baseline is like the ground on which the writer stands: When one walks or stands on level ground, one has good footing and is, therefore, secure and stable; uneven ground takes away from one's footing and makes for less stability. Extremely uneven ground may make it necessary to watch for sudden changes in the terrain in order to keep one's balance. How a person adheres to his writing's baseline reveals how flexible he is, how predictable he is and how straightforward or rigid he can be.

A rising handwriting, one which moves away from the line of writing in an upward direction, generally denotes a tendency towards excess energy and an attitude of optimism. Writing that adheres rigidly to a straight baseline, however, is not generally a positive indication. Such an inflexible line suggests a writer with an iron will who feels an unconscious need to carefully control his emotions. The maximum level of this type of handwriting is found when, if a line is drawn underneath it, the script is seen to keep perfectly in line. Such rigid writers can hardly be called spontaneous or flexible. This type of writing is usually typical of balanced, self-controlled people. Therefore, some flexibility in the line of writing is a positive indication. A supple baseline (as long as it does not become erratic) implies flexibility in the writer's life, an ability to adjust to situations that arouse feeling, a willingness to experience emotion and healthy spontaneity.

Too much variability in the line of writing points toward a person of very changeable or somewhat unstable emotions, someone whose footing is less than secure. A wavering baseline indicates that the writer is sensitive to events and circumstances and may be on an emotional roller coaster ride. Handwriting that constantly falls below the line of writing reveals someone who lacks positive or appropriate emotional control and who has a tendency to be easily discouraged. The extent to which the writing falls or rises also must be considered in the analysis.

TOOLS OF THE WRITER

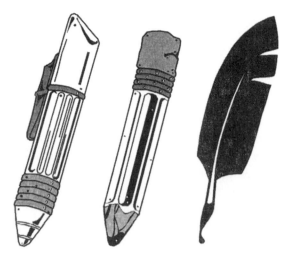

Check the tool you chose to use to write your sample. The instrument a person selects tells a great deal about his personality.

If he chooses a pencil, chances are he wants no firm commitments, nothing in black and white. Pencils can erase; they leave no evidence and suggest indecisiveness. A computer analyst, engineer, or CPA is likely to choose a fine ball-point pen because they are generally precise and want their writing clear and legible.

Those who select a broad, felt-tipped pen want to leave their mark. Excessively large writers, who cover the entire page, not only want to leave their mark, but also to get the most amount of mileage for the least amount of work. Writers who choose cartridge pens generally have good taste, enjoy music or the arts, and are often creative and appreciative of the appearance of the message on the page.

Given a choice of writing on lined or blank paper, people who choose to write on lined paper usually like to have structure in their lives and probably as a child enjoyed coloring and painting in coloring books. Writers who prefer unlined paper tend to be more independent, more spontaneous and generally like to live by their own rules.

Time Wars: Interpreting the Writer's Emotional Slant

The first item examined in a writing sample is the slant of the lettering. The slant reflects a person's underlying, inner emotional responsive characteristics. A writer's slant reveals how he reacts to other people and events in life. Slants range from extreme left to extreme right. Generally speaking, leftward slants signify emotional caution while rightward slants indicate unrestrained enthusiasm. A severe slant to the right indicates a sympathetic, emotional and sometimes impulsive nature. The more the letters lean to the right, the more emotional, vulnerable, outgoing and impulsive the writer is. Since he has the ability to sympathize, a person with this type of handwriting would side with the client who is at a disadvantage in a court case. The more solid and vertical a person's writing, the more rational and controlled he is. Vertical writing shows self-reliance, emotional control and a balance between extroversion and introversion. The farther writing leans to the left, the more private, self-absorbed and introverted the writer is.

To measure slant, one needs to calculate the angle of the upstrokes, the strokes that rise from the baseline. To help determine the average degree of the slant, use the Emotional Responsive Gauge below. A protractor from a stationery store can also be used to measure slant.

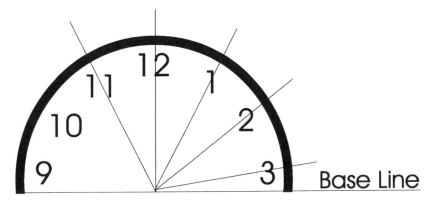

To determine slant, it will require at least 100 measurements. In order to measure correctly the slant of any letter, it must be firmly on the baseline. Slant lines can only be constructed, once baselines are determined. Notice how the measuring line rises from the baseline and travels straight through the top of the letter. Draw in slant lines in a different color ink than the one used in the writing sample. Start at the exact point where the letters begin to rise from the baseline and extend your slant line to the point at which the stroke stops going up and begins to come down.

To obtain true accuracy of the slant of writing, it is necessary to use the Emotional Gauge at all times. The gauge should be laid on the marked writing with the baseline of the gauge coinciding with the baseline of the letters being measured. Measurement should be recorded as shown in the example below.

TIME IS ON YOUR SIDE

Imagining the top half of a clock, an analysis of the various slants can be determined. If the slant is at:

11:00 o'clock:	Writing that registers 11:00 indicates one who is caring and responsive but has difficulty in showing it.
12:00 o'clock	Writing that registers 12:00 shows that judgment and analytical reasoning will rule the emotions. These writers are highly objective and logical.
1:00 o'clock	Writing that registers 1:00 indicates a quick, mild response of someone who is somewhat demonstrative.
2:00 o'clock	Writing that registers 2:00 is evidence of a moderately responsive nature of someone who is slightly sympathetic and extroverted.
3:00 o'clock	Writing that registers 3:00 is evidence of a high degree of responsiveness of someone who is emotional and demonstrative.
4:00 o'clock	Writing that registers 4:00 represents extreme responsiveness of someone who is too emotional and too sentimental.

| **11:00 to 4:00** | Writing that registers several degrees of responsiveness indicates varying emotional responses of someone who is quite unstable and completely unpredictable. |

In summary, the vertical writer will "look before leaping," and consider the benefits or advantages to be gained from any move. Emotional expression is a show of feeling and the farther the writing slants to the right, the more a person is likely to show how he feels. Therefore, when one finds writing that is slanting to the left on the Emotional Responsiveness Gauge, it is safe to determine that the writer does not show how he feels.

TIME WARS: THE PRESSURE'S ON

The pressure of a person's handwriting can tell a great deal about his level of intensity. A very heavy writer is extremely intense and is likely to pre-judge situations. A light writer, on the other hand, is more likely to be forthright. He expresses what he believes, gets it over with and goes on to the next item on the agenda. One always knows where one stands with a light writer. Light-pressure writers never get ulcers—they occasionally give them to the heavy writers.

Heavy writing (writing that can be felt on the reverse side of the page) reveals a person with a deeply emotional nature—one that will carry feelings, hurts or happiness, for a long period of time. Great intensity is revealed in heavy writing.

Shaded writing, with some strokes light and others extremely heavy, reveals a person who is deeply emotional and unpredictable.

Light line writing shows an individual who seems to ignore hurts or pleasures. He does not become saturated with either of these feelings so that they become part of his system. A light line writer will be hurt or pleased temporarily, in proportion to the lightness of the lines, the permanence of the emotion will be lessened.

In drawing comparisons between light and heavy writers, it is easy to acknowledge that these two writers may have a difficult time in understanding each other, as would far-forward-slant writers in understanding backhand writers. They are opposite in emotional makeup.

The heavy writer cannot understand how the light-line writer can change moods and recover so quickly. The latter cannot understand why the former is still carrying a grudge.

With what you have learned so far, see what makes you tick. Writing pressure, which signifies our internal clock, bears a striking similarity to the variety of timepieces we see around today.

The Grandfather clock: steady, dependable, reliable, well grounded and punctual is shown by writing that contains moderate pressure. This type of writing, like the sturdy Grandfather clock, shows solid movement and divine regalness. It is made of genuine wood and slowly prods its way along, quite like that of the vertical, judgmental 12:00 o'clock writer.

The Alarm clock: hyper, seldom relaxed, lives by the minute, is very regimented, is controlled by time, and always wound up, with its coil ready to snap. This is generally the very heavy writing that often tears through to the back of the page of a "Type A" (12:00 o'clock) personality who doesn't take time out to smell the roses. He is the type of person who would forgive his enemies, but never forget their names.

The Time bomb: ready to explode. This writing not only can be felt on the reverse side of the page, but also actually tears through the paper. This writer holds back his feelings, not knowing how to release them until he explodes. He keeps his alarm set and is often unpredictable, prejudiced and tends to live on the cutting edge. His general theory is, "Don't get angry. . . get even."

The Coo Coo clock: frivolous, basically upbeat, light, airy, not a lot of direction, scattered energy and sometimes flirtatious is set at 3:00 o'clock. This writer is usually a light writer who forms large letters, but uses small margins. This person is totally unpredictable and often out-of-control. He may be entertaining and the life of the party, but only for a short period of time. His writing tends to slant notably far to the right.

Are you a Digital clock with your battery running down? Perhaps you need to be recharged because your clock keeps going off at 2:00 a.m. It doesn't take much before you are back to normal. Just one positive happening and you are as good as new. This person applies average pressure in his writing and has a far right slant.

The Self-starter or stem winder writes straight up and down with a heavy hand, has exemplary initiative and finds it easy to get things going. This person gets moving on his own, sets his clock at 12 noon and is certain that all projects reach completion. He's eager to make his presence known.

A Pocket watch is extremely private. It's hidden in a pocket, protected by a cover that must be lifted in order to check what it has to say. This type of person wears his numbers close to his vest. His 11:00 o'clock slant writing is small and is done with average pressure. People have to make an effort to understand him. He has an idea of what other people are thinking, but few know what's on his mind, and that's the way he likes it. He doesn't like to be crowded and writes using wide spaces between his words.

Big Ben is ambitious, determined and part of the corporate structure. He has a tendency to take charge, lead others and his 12:00 o'clock up and down writing tends to be heavy, blocked and forceful.

The Hourglass personality resembles the sands of time; that is, he has a tendency to procrastinate. He's compulsive, keeps checking his watch and feels that time is always running out; he functions best at the last minute. He doesn't like to be rushed, but can handle projects with time frames or time constraints. His flamboyant, curly writing is rather large as if it were flowing and is done with heavy pressure.

A Mickey Mouse watch is usually worn by someone who is packed with fun and is somewhat immature. His writing is large, light and seems to flow right off the paper. It's usually set at 4:00 o'clock and the wearer is frantic because time is running out. He's always afraid he won't have enough time to finish his projects.

BREATHING ROOM: SIZE AND SPACING OF WRITING

The size of the writing itself is important. Space, in this context, refers to the area left between letters, words, and lines; margins are the borders surrounding the writing matter on a page. Tiny writing is associated with extreme powers of concentration. This type of writer doesn't seek the limelight and except with close friends, is not very communicative. Small writers often have an academic mentality. They have a talent for detail and organization. This type of writing is often created by computer analysts, accountants and those who could—literally—fill out their income tax returns, unperturbed, in Grand Central Station.

The copy book style or average-sized writer adheres to custom and is in tune with life. Well-spaced letters that are well formed suggest clarity and absence of clutter. It shows good discipline and organization, order and composure.

The larger a person's writing, the more restless he is apt to be and the more "breathing" space he is likely to need. This type of writer needs to make an impression on others, enjoys attention and admiration and does not like to be alone. Extremely large writing indicates a person who converges on life with extroversion and extravagance. The excessively small writer approaches life with reclusiveness and modesty. The attention span of the larger writer is usually not as great as that of the person with tiny writing. An attorney whose case will depend on a juror's comprehension of a great many details will fare better with jurors who write small, possess a long attention spans and have a rapt fixation for trivialities.

Spacing of Letters within Words

Spacing of letters within words is not revealing. Imagine a tight fist clutching gold dust and nothing slipping out; thus the less likely the individual will be to share his problems or wealth with others. As one relaxes the grip, a little gold dust sifts through; where one is judiciously sharing with others. When the fist is opened all the gold dust falls out; hence, easy come, easy go.

If an individual makes narrow letter forms, he can be expected to be narrow-minded about himself, judgmental, uptight, or self-conscious. If he makes broad letter forms, he can be expected to be inwardly broad-minded with himself, generously giving himself room to be natural and to grow.

The distance that the writer places between his written letters shows how he relates on a personal level to other people. If he is cautious or introverted, his letters will be crowded close to each other, though he may actually desire contact with others. Exceptionally narrow letter spacing indicates that the writer is fearful of making contact and cautious with his feelings.

If the writer is outgoing, expansive, and is not inhibited by others, it will be reflected in his wide letters with average spacing. This person is outgoing, generous, extroverted and people oriented. These writers feel at ease with themselves and are willing to share thoughts and feelings with others. Often they are extravagant or impulsive.

Spacing between Words

The space left between written words represents the distance that the writer would like to maintain between himself and society at large. Once again, as with the single letter, the writer is representing himself as he places each word unit on the page. Between his words, he sets the distance he needs for emotional comfort with others; it represents his territorial boundaries.

Extremely narrow spaces between words show someone who will crowd others for attention, constantly craving contact and closeness. Such a writer can be selfish in his demands and unwilling to give of his own time and energies to others.

Large, wide spaces between words indicate the writer's need to maintain a distance in a social atmosphere, either due to an inner need for privacy or to a tendency toward isolation sometimes reinforced by difficulty in communicating with others.

The combination of wide letters with wide spaces between the words denotes a person who demands attention in an extravagant or exaggerated manner, stemming from a need to be noticed, to be important.

Well-balanced spacing always gives evidence of the writer's social maturity, intelligence, and inner organization. This writer is able to deal flexibly and objectively with himself and with other people.

Spacing between Lines

Line spacing is by no means accidental. It is the subconscious intention of the writer. Since we place each line on the page one by one, they represent our need for organization. If the page represents a person's time frame, how he fills and organizes that page, shows how he paces himself.

The writer who positions his writing well on the page, moving unswervingly line after line across the page, is likely to go unhesitatingly about his tasks in an orderly manner. It is likely that his other traits will support this evidence of maturity and control.

The amount of space that the writer leaves between the lines on the page gives clues to the orderliness and clarity of his thinking, and to the amount of interaction that he wishes to have with his environment. Normal spacing has its own personal harmony and flexibility.

The more crowded and tangled a line is within itself or with those above and below, the more confused are the writer's thoughts and feelings. The inner pressure of many emotional reactions puts this type of individual in constant need of expressing himself in words, actions or projects. Such writers are lively, forceful and often creative, but can suffer from a lack of clarity of purpose or from jumbled ideas and poor concentration. It can be concluded that such a writer would behave in a disorganized, inconsistent manner, letting things happen instead of making things happen. His thoughts generally are scattered and he always has too many irons in the fire.

The writer who sets his lines far apart from each other on the page is isolating himself from his environment—socially, psychologically, or both. He has grown to fear contact and closeness, or he may have constructed grandiose fantasies for himself that set him apart from others, or he may harbor suspicions and hostilities that keep him separate and untrusting. Distance between lines is also an indication of extravagance, just as crowding can mean stinginess.

Rigid and Irregular Spacing

Rigid, machine-like placement of letters, words, and lines on a page indicates conscious or subconscious overcontrol on the part of a writer who is in fear of losing domination of himself or of his surroundings. He hides behind a carefully arranged facade of "beautiful" letter forms and planned spaces.

Irregular spacing on a page is a clue to an inwardly unsettled character in conflict with its social self, friendly one minute and withdrawn the next. Such a person has little sense of social boundaries and is usually unaware of his mood swings. Uneven spacing that leads to tangled words and lines are indicative of a writer who struggles with inner confusion, who lacks objectivity and organization, and who places heavy emphasis upon fantasy.

Excessive wide spaces between lines indicate the writer to be anything but frugal. Extremely wide spaces between words indicate a desire to be socially isolated.

INSTANT PEOPLE-READING THROUGH ANALYZING MARGINS

Narrow Margins Both Sides	Uneven Left Margin	Uneven Right Margin
Look as you've never looked before and you'll see as you've never seen before. Judge the Jury. Look as you've never looked before and you'll see as you've never seen before. Judge the Jury. Look as you've never looked before and you'll see as you've never seen before. Judge the Jury. Look as you've never looked before and you'll see as you've never seen before. Judge the Jury.	Look as you've never looked before and you'll see as you've never seen before. Judge the Jury. Look as you've never looked before and you'll see as you've never seen before. Judge the Jury. Look as you've never looked before and you'll see as you've never seen before. Judge the Jury. Look as you've never looked before and you'll see as you've never seen before. Judge the Jury.	Look as you've never looked before and you'll see as you've never seen before. Judge the Jury. Look as you've never looked before and you'll see as you've never seen before. Judge the Jury. Look as you've never looked before and you'll see as you've never seen before. Judge the Jury. Look as you've never looked before and you'll see as you've never seen before.
Lacks consideration for other people's space and is somewhat reserved.	*Disregard for balance or societal rules. May be rebellious or defiant.*	*Prone to mood swings. Lack of consistency in planning ahead. Impulsive at times.*

No Margins Anywhere

Look as you've never looked
before and you'll see as you've
never seen before. Judge the Jury.
Look as you've never looked
before and you'll see as you've
never seen before. Judge the Jury.
Look as you've never looked
before and you'll see as you've
never seen before. Judge the Jury.
Look as you've never looked
before and you'll see as you've
never seen before. Judge the Jury.
Look as you've never looked
before and you'll see as you've
never seen before. Judge the
JuryLook as you've never looked
before and you'll see as you've

*Excessively talkative,
fears solitude and
causes strong negative
or positive reactions
in others.*

Wide Upper Margin

Look as you've never looked
before and you'll see as
you've never seen before.
Judge the Jury. Look as
you've never looked before
and you'll see as you've
never seen before. Judge the
Jury. Look as you've never
looked before and you'll see
as you've never seen before.
Judge the Jury. Look as
you've never looked before
and you'll see as you've

*Extremely formal.
Respects authority,
is considerate of others
and is somewhat reserved.*

Narrow Upper Margin

Look as you've never looked
before and you'll see as
you've never seen before.
Judge the Jury. Look as
you've never looked before
and you'll see as you've
never seen before. Judge the
Jury. Look as you've never
looked before and you'll see
as you've never seen before.
Judge the Jury. Look as
you've never looked before
and you'll see as you've
never seen before. Judge the

*Indifferent and informal
toward others; directness
of approach.*

Wide Lower Margin

Look as you've never
looked before and you'll
see as you've never seen
before. Judge the Jury.
Look as you've never
looked before and you'll
see as you've never seen
before. Judge the Jury.
Look as you've never
looked before and you'll

*Highly reserved, aloof,
possible fear of emotional
attachment.*

Narrow Lower Margin

Look as you've never looked
before and you'll see as
you've never seen before.
Judge the Jury. Look as
you've never looked before
and you'll see as you've never
seen before. Judge the Jury.
Look as you've never looked
before and you'll see as
you've never seen before.
Judge the Jury. Look as
you've never looked before
and you'll see as you've never
seen before. Judge the Jury.
Look as you've never looked
before and you'll see as

*Sentimental, materialistic
with an intense desire to
communicate and a need
to stay with the familiar.*

Picture Perfect Margin

Look as you've never looked
before and you'll see as
you've never seen before.
Judge the Jury. Look as
you've never looked before
and you'll see as you've
never seen before. Judge the
Jury. Look as you've never
looked before and you'll see
as you've never seen before.
Judge the Jury. Look as
you've never looked before
and you'll see as you've
never seen before. Judge the
Jury. Look as you've never

*Well balanced,
responsible, excellent
organizational abilities.*

We are inclined to take margins left around writing for granted. If we give them any thought at all, it may be simply to consider them as a form for the written material—a way of setting it off pleasantly. Margins originated from the attempts of monks and scribes to keep the pages of their beautifully lettered manuscripts clean. By leaving a blank area at the side of the parchment, the writer (and later the reader), could place his thumb and forefinger on the page without soiling or smudging the heavy inks used to create the writing.

In general, a writer's appreciation for beauty is shown by form, balance and proportion. Writers of well-balanced pages may not possess actual skill in expressing themselves in an art medium, but they maintain a keen appreciation of art. Imbalance of margins created by disorderly writing, on the other hand, shows someone with little regard for orderliness, balance and proportion.

The page is space, and the way that an individual fills his page with script shows how he will approach the world and his space in life. A broad overall margin denotes refinement and taste. The writer usually paces himself and acts rather than reacts. The left side of the paper represents the past from which the writer starts, from which he makes his entrance into the environment. The right side symbolizes his goals and his future. Placement of writing on a page also shows the quality of the writer's taste, his social, cultural and artistic tendencies, or a lack of these. Subconscious feelings toward space and its use gives clues to a person's self-esteem and how he relates to others.

Balanced margins: This writer has an awareness of social boundaries, poise, order, and control. He is well balanced and maintains an aesthetic sense.

Wide left margin: This writer makes an extravagant beginning at the left margin and begins to crowd and reduce his letters in size as he approaches the right margin. The naturally expansive person seems to be overcome with regret for his wastefulness and tries to compensate for it. He displays an avoidance of the past, willingly communicates with others and possesses courage in facing life. The person who crowds his letters and words at the end of a line, may splurge with dollars when he has them, then pinch pennies to exist.

Wide right margin: A frugal person will feel that economical use of the page is important and will begin writing at the extreme left edge. This type of person is inclined to conserve his emotional, mental and material resources. He has a fear of the future, is over sensitive, self-conscious and reserved.

Wide margins all over: This person is withdrawn and aloof, is sensitive to color and form in surroundings. He places a huge importance on money and is somewhat artistic.

Left margin widening: This writer is eager to move away from the past world and is optimistic and impatient.

Left margin narrowing: This person shows inner fatigue or depression caused by haste or overwork. He finds it hard to let go of the past.

Narrow margins both sides: Shows stinginess or acquisitiveness and a lack of consideration and reserve. These writers usually have full schedules and check their calendars before accepting dates. They take advantage of spare moments, rarely taking time to relax.

Uneven left margin: Signifies defiance and rebellion toward the rules of society on the part of the writer. It also divulges a lack of inner order and balance in most matters.

Uneven right margin: This writer displays impulsive moods and his acts and reactions are unreliable.

No margins anywhere: Shows a person who eliminates all barriers between himself and others. He is apt to cause strong negative or positive reactions in others and usually talks too much. He tends to fear empty spaces or death.

Wide upper margin: Modesty, formality and respect are being shown toward the person being written to. The writer may be timid. In old English culture, the amount of space at the top of the page indicated the rank of the person to whom it was addressed.

Narrow upper margin: Indicates informality, directness of approach, a lack of respect and indifference. Writers who start at the very top of the page have a casual approach to life and relationships; and they aim to say, "Make way for my ideas."

Wide lower margin: Shows someone who is losing interest in his own environment. It indicates idealism, aloofness, and a person extremely reserved in his behavior style.

Narrow lower margin: Discloses a person with a desire to communicate, who is sentimental and sometimes depressed. It also indicates a person who is beset with materialism.

YOUR SCRIPT IS SHOWING

Obviously, no single characteristic of a writing sample is necessarily bad in every case. A graphoanalyst must examine and break down all handwriting strokes until the total picture emerges. When used this way, handwriting analysis can serve as a technique for attorneys to use to gain better insights into a prospective juror's personality and quirks. It can be used to determine the emotional stability of the writer and tells whether the writer is tolerant or narrow-minded. The juror's handwriting also provides the attorney with knowledge concerning the juror's outlook on life. Is he an optimist or a pessimist? Does he have a poor concentration span and a tendency to become restless, or a long attention span and an ability to sit for long hours sifting through detailed evidence? These tell-tale signs are found throughout the potential juror's handwriting and can serve as a powerful instrument in final decisions concerning selection.

Time is the essence of life. If you waste your time, you waste part of your life. The time saved in analyzing the handwriting of a potential friend, mate, business associate or jury member is the "watch of a winner." Indecision is an assassin. Instead, make better choices and wiser decisions. Then, time becomes your ally, your valuable partner. When you master your time, you master your destiny.

Saving 1 hour per day gives you an extra 9 weeks per year.

Saving 30 minutes per day gives you an extra 4½ weeks per year.

Saving 15 minutes per day gives you an extra 2½ weeks per year.

A PERSONAL NOTE . . . ALICE

After reading the newspaper coverage and listening to the local television stations night after night give details concerning the destructive behavior of Angel Maturino Resendez, alias Rafael Resendez-Ramirez (The Rail Car Killer), I was hoping to get the opportunity to see and analyze his writing for personal and educational purposes.

I got that opportunity and was asked to conduct the analyzation for personality traits that might prove helpful to local and national police officials in siting him or determining his location. I carefully studied the 12 signatures in front of me, knowing well that a signature is a person's psychological calling card or his trademark that he wants to share with others. Because all the signatures were copied and faxed, I was limited in my findings, however; I could ascertain that he felt very comfortable with the first name, but severely uneasy with his last name, perhaps because he had so many aliases.

His signature was full of deception, manipulation and evasiveness. His writing showed that he is a person who is a compulsive liar, who pauses to cover his tracks the same way that he pauses in his writing, retracing certain letters.

The sweeping stroke that Angel Maturino Resendez makes over his entire signature, which is superfluous and is his true trade mark, is designed for all to see his flair for showmanship and his craving to be the star who takes over all of the news media. Just as Zorro left his mark, so has The Rail Car Killer!

Let Your Fingers Do the Talking

Improvement begins with "I".

You can learn more about yourself and others from the lower-case *t* than from any other single letter because the way you write your *t* is the way you set your game plan for life. This letter can have long strokes, short strokes, heavy strokes or light strokes. Some strokes might even start light and grow thicker, while others start thick and grow lighter.

Since the lowercase *t* can be written in many different ways, it allows for a variety of personal expressions. With the small *t* there is a stem. A *t* stem can be tall or short, begin below the line of writing or above it or can be heavy and dark or light and airy. All of these variations provide an opportunity for the analyst to determine the truth about the writer's character traits, namely: vanity, pride, sensitivity, enthusiasm, persistence, and ambition.

The *t* cross can also take on many variations in length, heaviness and placement on the stem. It may cross the stem half way up, or it may even cross entirely above the stem itself. The cross bar may be light or heavy, long or short or there may be no cross at all. The cross bar may not be a bar at all, but a tied stroke. The *t* cross reveals important information about the writer, such as his: goals, self-esteem, self-confidence, plans, intentions and accomplishments.

YOUR WRITING FITS YOU TO A *T*

First, consider the height of the *t* and *d* stem in relationship to the other baseline letters. The normal height of the *t* stem is about two and one-half to three times that of the small letters. This height implies that the writer stands tall with pride, has a healthy sense of self-satisfaction where goals and accomplishments are concerned and possesses an average level of self esteem. A stem above the average height indicates vanity; exceedingly tall *t* stems show extreme vanity, or pride gone wild.

The extremely tall stem writer who retraces the stem feels he is much better on his job than others. He is often over confident and impressed with himself. The short *t* stem writer thinks and acts for himself and doesn't need other people's approval. He is not bothered by customs and will only conform to dress or other requirements if it is absolutely necessary.

Stems that are short represent various degrees of independent thinking and independent people. They are usually leaders and often break boundaries to get a job done. These types of writers are not good "yes" men and they do not necessarily expect others to agree with them. The line going up when making a *t*, represents the writer's pride. Retracing that line and returning to the base line represents the writer's dignity. When one bends his pride and dignity by adding a loop, he has indicated a sensitivity to criticism. The rules that apply to *t* stems, also apply to *d* stems as well.

Loops found in a *t*-stem refers to the writer's accomplishments. Loops found in the *d*-stem apply more to a personal sensitivity to criticism. The trait of sensitivity to criticism can also make one sensitive to other people's feelings, but when it is exaggerated, it can be negative.

T-Cross Placement

T-bars can be above the stem, they may be high on the stem, average on the stem or even placed fairly low on the stem. It is their location that is important. The *t*-bar may be long, short or medium in length. It may be heavy or light. It may be written ahead of the stem or following it. A relatively heavy *t*-bar shows purpose, or expresses one's will power. A light cross-bar shows a purpose that has less force behind it. The aspiration may exist, but the force of the purpose is light, not clearly defined and the writer will be less likely to carry it out.

When *t*-bars are long, they represent carrying power and action. They not only cross the stem but they continue to move, and in the language of the graphoanalyst, they represent enthusiasm.

Cross bars that appear level or almost level with the tops of small letters are evidence of the fact that the writer is practical, conservative and not a risk taker. He will never gamble the family fortune. He sets goals lower than that of what he is probably capable of doing. A cross bar placed slightly higher on the stem or in the middle of the *t*, reveals a person who can make long-range plans, but still be realistic and practical.

On the other hand, the writer who places the cross-bar near the top of the *t* stem is shooting at a distant or visionary goal. He is looking ahead, striving for a more distant purpose. When the cross-bar is heavy, he knows exactly where he is going and has the will power to achieve his goals. When it is light, he does not have as clearly defined an intent, but he still has a distant purpose. The height of the *t*-bar determines the writers level of setting goals, and the heaviness or weight of the stroke identifies how clearly his purpose is defined in his thinking.

The cross-bar written above the *t* stem shows a writer who sets impractical goals. When the line is light, the goal is usually not practical. It depicts a writer who sees a distant goal, dreams about it, but does not have a definite purpose to achieve it. When a writing sample shows *t*-bars crossed at different levels, there is evidence that the writer is a visionary and a combination of all of the above.

A *t* bar may be compared to a crow bar—when it is bent in an arc (turned down), it expresses strong self control. When it is in the reverse arc position, the writer may be a shallow thinker.

When the cross is made following the *t*, and is long enough to cover the width of three ordinary letters, it is an indication that the writer has a tendency to think faster than he's going. This may also indicate one with a temper. *T*-bars made before the stem show procrastination. The person tends to postpone or prioritize, promising himself he will get to it later.

How Do You Communicate?

Communication plays a vital role in our interpersonal relationships. When the parties involved are open and honest, the friendship can usually succeed. How one communicates is shown primarily in the formation of his circle letters, especially *a*'s, *o*'s, *g*'s and *d*'s. These letters show if the writer is frank, deceptive, manipulative, secretive, reserved or talkative.

Frankness, Talkativeness and Secretiveness

Frankness is evident in the circle formations of the *a*, *o*, *g*, and *d*. Clear, open and rounded circles, without extraneous loops (when no loops or hooks are evident in the circle structure) or marks, illustrates frankness, the willingness to be honest and communicate clearly what is on your mind. Clear circles indicate a lack of secretiveness, concealment or deceit and are a major component of integrity and dependability.

Circle letter closed at the top suggest one who is a good confidant. The writer is somewhat reserved, and is not readily communicative. If the letter is open at the mouth, the writer is inclined to be talkative. Think of these letters as open mouths that are ready to reveal what is on their minds.

No trait wears one hat. It is good to be generous unless you are a loan officer or a credit manager. It may be wise to be secretive if you are a doctor or an attorney.

Secretiveness implies that the person deliberately withholds information as a means of self-protection, perhaps as a result of deception, but always from a strong need for privacy. Secretiveness is indicated when a final loop closes the circle letter structure to the right. If the circle is closed, he has achieved the ability to keep things to himself and perhaps be diplomatic.

The secretive individual conceals personal information. He may talk all around it, but does not mention it. He tells only what he wants others to know. The facts he conceals may be unimportant, but because they are so personal in nature, he has classified them as private. Secretive writers sometimes need to be drawn out and they usually make good confidants.

Directness and Decisiveness

When the initial upward stroke of a letter structure is omitted and the writer begins the letter with a downward stroke, the trait of directness is evident. This type of writer has the ability to come straight to the point. He wastes no time on irrelevant thoughts or details and approaches a problem directly, never deviating from his line of thought. He appreciates simplicity and explicitness rather than elaboration. Directness is shown in several letter formations, some of which are *t*, *f*, *h*, and *b*.

Decisiveness is reflected in firm endings and final strokes of letters and words. This type of person has the ability to come to a definite decision with certainty and resoluteness. He can terminate a situation or controversy without much anxiety. The indecisive person has a fear of making decisions or coming to a conclusion, therefore, he will form letters that contain weak ending strokes. He tends to fluctuate between possible choices because he fears the results involved in a decision. Indecisiveness weakens the whole character structure of a person.

Stubbornness

The stroke formation that represents stubbornness is a wedge formed (similar to a teepee) by an upward stroke and a downward stroke. It is sometimes evident in the formation of an individual's *t*. These people usually have their minds made up in one certain way and will not give in, or budge, for anyone or anything.

Are You Open-minded?

The *e* is a very personal letter. Though the *a* and *o* show how well we communicate, the *e* indicates what we do with what we take in. For example, a closed *e* similar to an *I* depicts one who has a closed mind. A slender opening in the *e* shows one who will listen to everything, but at one point he may think, "Well, I have heard everything, but the bank is closed to deposits." He will then make the final decision. An *e* that is inflated depicts one who is gullible. A combination of *e* structures, indicates one who will listen, sift out the important information and then act accordingly.

If you are open-minded, the circle letters of your writing, especially the *e*'s, will be well-rounded. Rounded *e*'s are indicative of a person who is open to new ideas and approaches. He is the type of person who is willing to listen to advice before coming to a final conclusion, he possesses a broad-minded attitude that allows for possibilities outside his own thinking. This individual displays consideration for others and aids projects in a cooperative manner.

A narrow-minded attitude is reflected in tight, narrow *e* structures, indicating that the writer is closed to ideas or approaches other than his own. The narrow-minded person's mind is already made up. If several *e*'s are open and some are closed, it indicates that the writer will listen to everything, but basically he will make his own decisions.

Persistence

Persistence is evident if a writer makes tied strokes in such letters as *f*, *t*, and *g*. Tied strokes appear as if a line is tied back through the stem of the letter. The person who writes in this manner will never admit defeat. Circumstances may cause delays in his plans or projects, but sooner or later he will pick up where he left off. He feels a deep desire to succeed and persists in achieving his goals and objectives despite the circumstances.

Perfectionism

The person who strives for perfection will dot his *i*'s and *j*'s and cross his *t*'s meticulously, paying close attention to details. His letter forms will be carefully made with uniform base lines and flawless spacing. His writing will be neat and orderly. Lines, margins and spacing will be exact. In effect, the perfectionist probably conforms strictly to all rules and customs concerning writing—and perhaps also follows this routine in his daily life.

A dot—no matter what kind—placed very close to the point of the *i* or *j* is evidence of care in regard to details. This close dotting of the *i* or *j* is an indication of the writer's good memory and that he pays special attention to every detail of a story or an item. The *i*-dot made to the left of the stem indicates procrastination. Loyalty to one's beliefs is registered by firm, round dots above the *i* and *j* in a writing sample.

Irritability

The *i*-dot, when excessively written as a slash, indicates a temper on the part of the writer. The arrow point indicates not only impatience, but sarcasm as well. The sarcasm is verified and supported if the writer's *t*-bars are arrow-like. A light dot made like an arrow means minor irritability, the kind that is felt rather than expressed.

Idiosyncrasy, the tendency of a person to respond to certain situations in an odd, unconventional or otherwise individualistic manner, can be found in writing where circles are used to dot the small letters *i* and *j*. This stroke indication may be supported by unusual formations elsewhere in the writing. Whenever a sample contains *i*-dot circles, know that you are dealing with an individual who wants to be unique and who does not want to be a statistic.

Temper

The *t*-bar in an individual's writing will give evidence of his temper. If the *t*-bar is very light and short, the writer is easily irritated. Such writers have an inclination to express their annoyance and then promptly forget it. The heavier the stroke, the more enduring the temper.

Imagination

Whenever there is a loop present in a writing sample, there's evidence that some form of imagination is present. Whether it's above or below the baseline, its structure is the same. Loops below the line are indicative of material imagination; the writer has the ability to find new applications for old subjects or materials. Loops above the line have to do with abstract concepts; the writer has the capacity to understand philosophical, spiritual and theoretical principles.

Long lower loops are evidence of restlessness and reveal a desire for change and variety. If the loops are wide as well as long, the writer has a variety of interests. He has a diversity of experiences and friends and enjoys sharing his happenings with them. Lower loops that are slender indicate a person who is careful in his selection of friends. Such writers will prefer to choose their friends according to some standard. That standard may be money, status, intelligence, profession, special interest or even temperament. This type of writer is also likely to limit his horizons to his own particular field.

Lower loops that are small and placed close to the bottom of the lower extension show clannishness in the writer. Clannishness is defined as "disposed to associate only with one's one clique." The trait refers to choice of friends; a restricted group, restricted even to the single personality of the writer without outside association. This type of writer is somewhat distrustful and tends to prefer social isolation. He makes friends easily on the surface and may know many people, but he does not include their acquaintances in his confidences.

When lower loops are not completed, meaning the stroke swings to the left but does not complete the loop, it indicates a writer who has imagination that is undeveloped or lacks direction and administration. He has the potential to imagine, but what he imagines lacks form or completeness. The lower loop is the structure that determines the writer's desire for companions, therefore, the reversal of this structure is indicative of a desire to avoid such associations.

THINKING ABOUT THINKING: WHAT MAKES UP YOUR MIND?

It is important to know the methods a person employs in thinking, how mentally alert he is and how he attempts to solve his problems. Individuals have varying mental capabilities, differing mental processes and thinking styles. The more active one's thinking, the more quickly the desire to express ideas. Further, few people employ only one method for problem solving, rather they use one dominant procedure and modify it with a lesser active one.

Graphoanalysts endorse four main mental processes: cumulative, investigative-exploratory, analytical, and comprehensive (instinctive).

Cumulative

Careful, methodical thinkers who tend to look at things from a conventional standpoint form "copy-book" writing letters. The tops of the *m*'s and *n*'s are usually well rounded, the *r*'s are broad-topped, and the circle letters are broad. These writers who are comfortable with the familiar and generally do not like to threaten the status quo by trying new and different things, still form their letters with the slowly written arches that they were taught in elementary school penmanship classes.

This writer likes to think by building one fact upon another to reach a conclusion and tends to continue this pattern in his writing. Similar to a mason, he adds each stone carefully to his structure, firmly grounding it, before another is put in place. He uses a slow process, but a sure one. This type of person accepts facts and proceeds to build his knowledge; he doesn't jump to conclusions.

Since this type of person thinks in a slow, methodical manner, he is sometimes misunderstood. When answering questions, because he takes his time, some may judge him as mentally slow. But, in actuality, he is typically the person who gets the answer correct. This careful, orderly pattern suggests someone who has creative ability and superb manual dexterity.

Investigative-Exploratory

The person who employs this mental pattern has to find out everything for himself. If he sees a sign that reads, "Do Not Touch," he must touch to feel the texture of the object. If someone tells him of a new, exciting restaurant, he wants to go himself. He does not want cliff notes about a book, he wants to read the entire novel. It is not that he does not believe, it is only that it is his nature to want to experience through exploration.

This type of person's writing is characterized by upward pointed wedges instead of rounded tops. He has an insatiable curiosity, enjoys digging things out and he doesn't want help. The writer whose wedges are slender and sharp searches deeply; he wants to learn and investigate all that he can about a subject.

Analytical

The analytical thinker ponders, filters, weighs and evaluates information determining its value or worth to himself. This pattern of writing is recognized by the presence of wedges pointed toward the baseline. The sharper the wedge, the more thorough and complete the analysis.

This type of writing is frequently combined with the cumulative pattern; with the writer possessing both collected, methodical thinking and logical, sound reasoning. In such a case, rounded m and n segments will be separated by a spreading wedge, thus indicating analytical thinking ability. This process of writing slows down thinking even more, and indicates the writer's ability to evaluate whatever he uncovers.

Comprehensive (Instinctive)

The individual who is quick to understand people and situations and able to make snap decisions writes by making needle-like upward points, most frequently in the m's and n's that are similar to inverted v's. These are individuals whose mental processes are so rapid that they defy attempts to detect the steps by which they arrive at conclusions. This type of person has an immediate grasp of a situation or idea, in fact, his thinking seems to be effortless. The taller and more pointed the structures are, the quicker is his comprehension of ideas.

This writer feels he needs little explanation for anything and acutely aware of both people and surroundings. Shrewd comprehension has its pit-falls, because sometimes the thinker is too likely to rely on quick impressions not substantiated by more careful thought processes and consequently forms inaccurate judgments.

People who display a variety of mental processes in their writing sample are well equipped for problem solving. The writer is sometimes quick and adaptable or at others he may be indefinite and uncertain. Usually a combination of two or more thinking styles is beneficial, giving the person various ways of looking at situations and dealing with every day life. A singular style gives a more one-sided approach.

THE THREE ZONES OF HANDWRITING: MIDDLE, UPPER AND LOWER

Predominant Upper Zone

take time to think

Predominant Middle Zone

take time to think

Predominant Lower Zone

my time mostly

Handwriting is basically divided into three zones. A spatial analogy to this would be a tree, with its branches and leaves reaching into the sky, the playground of the mind and abstract thought, its trunk thrusting out of the baseline earth, the area closest to the concerns of human endeavor, and the root system reaching unseen below representing energy in the area of instinctual drives. Good growth balance between branches, trunk and roots promises that the tree/writer can withstand many a storm.

The middle zone is that of the mundane (down to earth) or daily living. It usually contains the lower case letters, and from this area the extender letters have their origin. This area represents the writer's thinking, his habitual ideas, his ability to accept ideas and to communicate them and his ability to interact with others.

In seeking expression, the mind tends to reach upward out of the common sphere of daily existence into the unknown. For this reason, the upper zone is called the area of the abstract. Indications of the writer's future, his daydreams and his capacity to deal with philosophies, theories, the spiritual, in fact, all his intangible qualities of life are found in this area. The height to which the structures reach indicates the degree of the writer's ability to understand or perhaps pursue such subjects.

The lower zone reflects our physical desires, our unconscious need for friends and our monetary aspirations. It is our action area and in it exists our qualities of determination and material imagination. This area also contains indicators of the writer's desire for change, travel and variety.

When the zonal dimensions are well-balanced and in good form, the writer shows stability at the most basic level, as well as involvement and initiative, and is essentially stable. He can handle his own thoughts and feelings, easily expresses himself and generally accomplishes his goals. Well-balanced zonal writing shows a writer with a combination of capabilities to handle the abstract, as well as, the mundane and to possess a sense of determination with a deep desire to communicate his ideas.

The writer who keeps the majority of his letters in the middle zone is one who is overly concerned about today and his own mundane activities. He does not possess deep insight into abstract subjects. He tends to underrate himself and may sometimes suffer from inferiority problems. He is basically living in a today world for "me" only.

YOUR SIGNATURE: THE FACE YOU SHOW THE WORLD

Signatures have always been recognized as unique and personally expressive. And are indicative of your public identity—the image you want other people to see. It can be considered your persona, as it is the face you show the world.

As an individualized symbol, your signature is a very personal trademark; it is recognized as yours alone, whether affixed to a check, a driver's license, a credit card or a legal document. The word signature comes from a Latin word meaning "to seal." By signing your name you declare yourself accountable for what you have signed. One's signature is legally binding because no one else can successfully duplicate it in all of its nuances.

As no prescribed standards govern signatures, you have unlimited freedom in creating your mark. Your signature may be clear and concise, legible or illegible, ornate or simple, underline, or followed by a dash or a dot.

Whatever stroke formations constitute the signature, it must never be analyzed apart from the text of the writing, which reinforces or modifies the signature's indications. Evaluation of the signature calls for the same principles that generally apply to handwriting and also the awareness that this is how the writer wishes to be *seen*, not necessarily who he or she really *is*. Zonal emphasis, stroke direction, slant, pressure, and spacing all apply, just as they do to other writing.

Perhaps the best-known signature in the United States is that of John Hancock, who said as he signed the Declaration of Independence, "King George can read that clear across the sea." To emphasize his statement, he added a bold, confident, somewhat showy flourish under his name.

A primary consideration is the clarity of the signature. If legible, it reveals straightforward communication based on a healthy self-concept. The writer of a clear signature does not need to make a pretentious display because he feels at ease with self, and does not make a chore or a guessing game out of reading his name or personality. A clear signature implies frankness and a consideration of others.

The signature that is simple and tastefully decorated with mild flourishes implies social demeanor, good taste, confidence and a healthy and expressive ego.

An illegible signature can be the result of an unwillingness to communicate clearly, an attempt to cover true thoughts and feelings, a belief that an embellished or bizarre signature is less likely to be forged, or a desire to impress. It is also important to consider whether the writer is required to sign his name many times a day and has therefore, developed an expedient, indecipherable way of doing so.

When the signature and text are similar in style, size, spacing, slant and zonal distribution, the writer's outward expressions reflect inner attitudes. Such writers are unpretentious and have no need to hide or mask their true natures.

When the signature and text are different, conflicts are suggested; the writer projects one thing but feels another. If the body of writing is small, he may hide behind the facade of a strong, bold signature to impress others with a show of confidence which may actually be a compensation for low self-esteem.

A small signature attached to larger text implies that the writer projects less self-importance than he or she really feels. The person is confident and self-reliant inside, but modest on the surface—perhaps even self-effacing if the signature is much smaller than the text.

A signature that is totally illegible signifies one who feels that he knows who he is and if others do not, that's their problem.

Please Sign In

Signatures are composed of up to four separate components: first name, middle name, last name and an underscore or flourish, which may all be executed in one movement or separated. The first name relates to the writer's ego and to feelings about self carried over from childhood. Therefore, when the first name is larger, clearer or otherwise more emphasized than the surname, the writer is independent of family or tradition, giving more importance to a feeling of individuality. This usually indicates self-reliance and a de-emphasis of prestige or social standing. The writer with an exaggerated first name may want to remain childlike or hold onto childish ways and ignore social considerations. An overly embellished first name reveals a craving for personal recognition beneath which may be a narcissistic attitude.

When family is emphasized, the person is dependent on status, family values, heritage and tradition. The writer may sacrifice the private, inner life to social prestige, power or business. A woman who writes her married name bolder or larger than her first name is likely to be secure with her husband and perhaps dependent on him. She likes being connected to his name and may even write, "Ms. John Smith" instead of "Jane Smith."

A signature underlined either by a continuation of the final stroke or by a separate line reveals independence, courage, self-worth and self-reliance. Such a writer believes in the self and personal accomplishment (if signs in the text also indicate confidence). The underscored signature is common to people who have achieved notoriety, as it is one sign that the person wishes to do something important.

Occasionally, a signature is partially or completely enclosed in a circle. This self-protective movement guards one's family status or the individual's own personal image or reputation, depending on which part of the signature is enveloped. The writer, by closing himself off, prefers to remain a mystery and does not want his privacy to be penetrated.

Signatures that are crossed out reveal that the writer is not happy with his or her own status quo or that of the family. The crossing out reveals an unconscious dislike for how things are and a desire to make a major change in life. This can also be an indication that the writer is self-driven and pushes himself to the limit.

Patched, or retraced to look better, letters in the person's name show inner anxiety and an uncertain self-concept. The writer, wanting to be seen as perfect, goes back to make repairs on the signature—the image the public sees. Patching may show that the writer dislikes and is trying to "fix" the self or how he is perceived.

Signatures are frequently graphic indications of what the writer identifies with—a profession or perhaps a special interest. Liberace, for example, signed his name with the drawing of a grand piano and a candelabra.

Forgery

The average amateur forger is one who attempts to copy a signature—not merely write it, but tries to follow a new trail of thought processes. He does not think like the writer whose signature he attempts to copy. It is very difficult to suddenly adopt all of the personality traits of another that it has taken that person a lifetime to build. The forger must put aside all of his own personality traits. There may be a slight change in the slant, the intensity of the writing or in the pen lift. There is no such thing as "the perfect forgery."

Signatures reveal the worst and the best of a writer's character and show the widest of variations. Since gender cannot be ascertained by writing alone, a signature on a document does provide confirmation of the writer's sex.

Bob Hope

Mother Teresa

Jerry Lewis

Donald Trump

The "Write" Person for the Right Job/Jury

Graphoanalysis is a practical, time-saving and dependable aid in person-nel selection and promotions. It is a proven method of personality assess-ment and is a supplement to, not a replacement for, conventional methods of hiring and upgrading. Ordinarily, records and documents are available of the applicant or jury member's education, training and experience, but not so easily attainable is pertinent information to quickly describe the subject's personality and potential. This gap in a candidate's background can be bridged through the knowledge obtained in his handwriting.

A graphoanalytical report reveals how the subject's personality traits match, or fail to match, the job requirements, or in the case of a courtroom situation, how the potential juror's traits match that of the "ideal" juror for a particular case. The report includes information on how the person being analyzed might be expected to relate with fellow employees, and lists a number of his strengths and weaknesses.

The mixture of strengths and weaknesses, present and potential, can spell success or failure for a candidate anticipated to work for a company or for a prospective juror expected to work with a case.

Corporate demand for handwriting analysis has doubled in the past years. It is the only non-discriminatory tool, since age, race, color, creed or religion cannot be determined from the handwriting sample. Studies obtained concerning employee compatibility to job success have shown an 80% accuracy.

The handwriting analyst doesn't make the final decision, his job is to point out the strong and weak traits of the candidate. European markets are just as interested in using graphoanalysis in the hiring of their personnel. The Wall Street Journal contends that the Parisians are familiar with screening job applicants by studying their penmanship. In fact, handwriting plays a much bigger part of business life in Europe than it does in the United States.

A hint to a job applicant that his handwriting may be scrutinized by an analyst is when there is a request for a handwritten letter to accompany his job application. When this happens, it is wise for the candidate to write in the manner he feels most comfortable, be it printing or writing.

From a handwriting sample, the analyst can ascertain if the applicant has the skills, the compatibility with concurrent employers and employees and the environmental compatibility to be successful in certain surroundings. The candidate's handwriting can indicate whether he prefers to be confined to a small area, or does he need a place to pace.

PUTTING THE PIECES (LETTERS) TOGETHER

An awareness of graphoanalysis not only enhances our ability to understand ourselves, but it also sheds light on business, social, courtroom and romantic relationships. By looking at ourselves honestly, we can deal more effectively with our weaknesses and build on our strengths. When we understand ourselves, we can better understand others and understanding others helps us to accept them as they are.

A stroke is a stroke, wherever you find it and an attorney who knows he is going to be involved in a lengthy and complicated trial might do well to choose a person who quite precisely dots his *i*'s and crosses his *t*'s. Through his knowledge of handwriting analysis, the attorney feels certain that this is the type of person who devotes an unusual amount of energy to details, who doesn't procrastinate and who would be apt to listen to every word of his client's testimony.

"The bottom line as I see it," says 'Racehorse' Haynes, "is that in jury selection you have to use as many advantages as possible, and social science and statistics in the courtroom are just the latest of our ever more sophisticated techniques. That does not mean that I would ever permit a social scientist to preempt my option to make the seat-of-the-pants, back-of-the-neck judgment based on everything I've learned and read in my career. The fact is, jury selection is still guesswork right down to the wire. The difference is that now jury selection is a little more intelligent guesswork."

Handwriting analysis is the piece of information that puts the entire puzzle successfully together.

KEYNOTE SPEAKERS OF THE ALPHABET

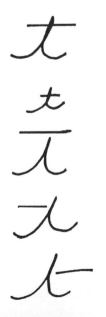

You are proud, dignified and enthusiastic.

You think for yourself. You are your own person.

You may be called a dreamer with "castles in the clouds."

There is a tendency to procrastinate or prioritize.

You have a propensity for thinking ahead of yourself.

You possess good initiative and would be a good team leader.

You are persistent and will "hang in there" until you get the job done.

As you remember events from your past, you may experience a bit of guilt or self-castigation.

You are direct and to-the-point.

You have the ability to move rhythmically from one project to another.

Being somewhat stubborn and inflexible, you hold firm to your beliefs.

You are struggling to exert self-control in a particular area.

You may not be serious enough in achieving your goals.

At times you may possess a domineering nature. You prefer instant gratification.

Because you are somewhat sensitive to criticism, you continuously try to put your best foot forward.

You are constantly braced for criticism even when it isn't going to occur.

You possess strong willpower in achieving your goals.

The height of the *t* and *d* stem in relation to the average height of the smaller (or mundane) letters indicates one's degree of pride. Two to 2½ times the size of the small letters depicts average self esteem. Any stem above that height indicates vanity. Stems that are short indicate independent thinking.

You are talkative, frank, open . . . hard put to keep a secret. You enjoy interaction with others.

You are broadminded, an exemplary confidant and somewhat reserved.

You are self-deceptive and tend to rationalize. You may try to say things in a positive way in order to avoid hurting one's feelings.

You are cautious and diplomatic.

You have a tendency to circumvent the truth and sometimes pause to cover your tracks.

The *o*'s and *a*'s are our conversational letters. When they are clear and void of unnecessary strokes, it is an indication that the writer is sincere.

The letter *e* is a personal letter and is indicative of what a person does with the information he absorbs.

You will listen to everything and form your own opinions.

If you have a combination of these *e*'s, you will listen, and at one point may feel that "you have heard everything and the bank is closed to deposits." You may then decide to do what you originally wanted.

Gullibility is pronounced. You could be a "sucker" for a sad story.

You possess a desire for culture. This is intensified if you have similar *r*'s.

You will listen to everything, even though you have already made up your mind.

You do not miss a detail when contemplating the solution to a problem. You can also recall facts easily.

You have a tendency to prioritize your time or delay unpleasant tasks.

You have the profound ability to walk into a room and quickly assess everything. Your family often thinks that you have eyes in the back of your head.

You may become impatient with details.

You have an intense desire to be unique, individualistic and not a statistic.

Often found in the writing of young people; says, "Like me, love me; I need your approval."

You tend to skim the surface and get just enough to "get by with."

You prefer to learn methodically . . . fact by fact and building one stone upon another.

Your keen comprehension enables you to learn easily. You prefer to do things for yourself.

You have an insatiable curiosity. If a sign reads "wet paint," you may be tempted to touch it.

You are determined and have the capability to move continuously toward your goals.

You are selective in choosing friends; they are few, but close.

You like to be with your friends, but you also enjoy your private time.

You choose your intimate friends carefully and share very little of your personal affairs. Some may view you as being clannish.

You have a limited number of friends and sometimes feel undeserving.

You enjoy people and like sharing your time.

You like to be surrounded by people and may be tempted to ask the "Avon lady" to lunch.

Very persistent; you will stay with the project until you achieve what you deserve.

Your memory for past events stays with you and causes you to have an occasional tinge of guilt.

You remember things from your past and benefit by each experience as you carry things into the future with enthusiasm.

You have talent or creativity lying dormant that is not presently being utilized.

You have the ability to go from one subject to another and also the craft to express ideas easily.

A PERSONAL NOTE . . . ALICE

While lecturing to a high school psychology class, I was asked by a student, "What can I do or undo through my handwriting that would help me feel better about myself?"

There is nothing I would propose or teach about trying to change your handwriting, hence . . . change your personality. It must be a reverse procedure. Once a trait changes in your personality, it is reflected in your handwriting.

I suggested the following exercise to the student, which had been proven to be successful. I advised her to write the phrase, "Take time to think," thirty times each evening before retiring for a period of thirty days. I instructed her to raise slightly higher and to extend the *t*-bar crosses in her writing. *T*-bar crosses placed high on the stem signify a writer who is confident and when *t*-bars are extended, it shows a writer who displays enduring enthusiasm.

Several months later I received a note from the young student telling me of her many successes, including her graduation from high school in the upper percentile of her senior class! Yes, the *t*-bar crosses in her note, were higher!

Don't Write Off Your Doodles

Life is the art of drawing without an eraser.

THE GET-TO-KNOW-YOURSELF QUIZ

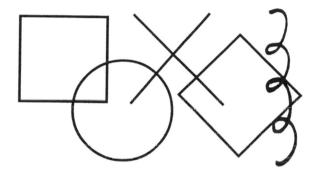

Your attraction to certain archetypal symbols—the circle, square, triangle, cross, and spiral—offers clues to your current psychological state. Draw the shapes shown above and then number them from one to five in order of preference— that is, your favorite shape will be one and your least favorite will be five. The meaning of each symbol is revealed at the end of this chapter.

So, you think all those loops, lines, circles, squares, and squiggles you doodle when you're on the phone or in a meeting are merely the products of a bored mind? You're absolutely wrong! Your scribbles actually tell you about your hidden desires, fantasies, fears, or even the way you cope with life in general.

HISTORICAL DEVELOPMENT OF ART EXPRESSION

Before humans developed the use of phonetic language, they used pictorial symbols to give permanence to their expression of communication. Works of art have long been catalogued in archeological investigations of societal development as examples of how early men and women attempted to produce expressions of ideas and emotions. Thus, drawings must be considered as the basis for elemental communication. Even in primitive times, men and women used etchings and carvings to express feelings and record actions. There is much evidence to suggest that the use of visual forms of art originally served functional purposes rather than merely aesthetic ones.

As it is often suggested that individual development reflects the development of the species, so is it that children learn to draw before they can write. Children first begin making scribbles at ages 2 and 3, drawings that are seen as purposeless expressions of activity that become more refined and differentiated. By age 4, single lines replace the unorganized scribble and by age 5 or 6, children begin to draw crude symbols representing people and animals. Ten and 11-year-old children are inclined to copy and trace the works of others, while 11- to 14-year-olds prefer drawing geometrical forms and decorations rather than human forms. Children's drawings develop in an orderly fashion. Consequently, all of those dots, lines and circles that display different muscular movement development, can be used by mental health professionals in obtaining a rich understanding of a child's intelligence and personality.

Freud hypothesized that symbols represent forgotten memories and Jung asserted that symbols are a personal experience only partially formed. Freud and Jung's explanations of the unconscious processes of the mind gave the users of art for psychotherapeutic purposes a foundation for diagnostic work that followed and paralleled psychoanalysis.

Expression through pictures is much more symbolic and less specific than words. increased memories and fantasies are more likely to result in a person's drawing than in his written work. Since drawings are less specific than words, they allow a person to communicate in a vague manner without having to acknowledge, for example, that the house in his drawing is not really where he lives.

Understanding the use of Drawings as Aids in the Assessment Process

Specifically trained art therapists look for symbols in drawn images and attempt to help clients become more cognizant of their inner selves. They then help their clients to integrate their newly discovered inner selves with their outer realties in the hope of enhancing their self-expression and understanding.

The use of color in drawings can be highly subjective in meaning. The excessive use of the color red is often thought to be associated with the feeling of anger. The continued use of primarily dark colors is usually considered to be associated with worry. An overabundant use of multiple bright colors suggests gaiety and spontaneity. When individuals tend to repeatedly use light, barely visible colors, there is a good possibility that they are attempting to hide their true feelings and their authentic personality.

Promotions and other important decisions are often based—at least in part—on the results of personality tests. Since an individual's drawing can also reveal distinct personality clues—extrovert vs. introvert, sensitive vs. practical, friendly vs. hostile, calm vs. excitable, adventurous vs. inhibited, conscientious vs. irresponsible, sociable vs. reclusive, realistic vs. paranoid, independent vs. helpless, easygoing vs. inflexible—it is relevant to study and analyze any and every scribble made by a possible jury member, possible employee or even a possible mate.

Common Drawings that Elicit Valuable Information

HOUSE-TREE-PERSON

The House-Tree-Person (H-T-P) drawing is used as a technique to aid in gathering data regarding an individual's degree of personality, attachment, maturity and efficiency. These three objects are chosen to be drawn because of their familiarity, their acceptance by persons of all ages, and their ability to stimulate a greater fund of associations in comparison to other objects. Besides their use in assessment, drawing of these objects have also been found to be useful as an appraisal device in screening applicants for employment, and as a research instrument to locate common factors in an identified sample.

A set of instructions is given which specifies that the examinee is requested to draw a house, a tree, and then a person, without any additional comments as to type, size, or condition. The ordering of the H-T-P always remains the same because this sequence is viewed as gradually more psychologically difficult, with the tree drawing and the human figure appearing the most likely to produce personal responses.

The House

The drawing of a house tends to elicit connections regarding the examinee's home and the interpersonal dynamics being experienced within the family setting. The house, it has been theorized, represents the place wherein affection and security are sought. In other words, a drawing of a chimney emitting smoke is often related to feelings of warmth and affection.

1. Details:

   (a) Essentials (normal drawing): At least one door, one window, one wall, a roof, a chimney.

   (b) The more items drawn on or around the house, the more content and secure the artist is with his family and his environment.

   (c) A house vacant of any type of adornment (a simple square drawn with a triangle above it) is equivalent to that of a home where there sometimes is a lack of attachment and affection among the people inside.

2. Chimney:

   (a) Symbolic of warm, intimate relations between the artist and his family members.

   (b) Absence of chimney: indicates a person who often experiences conflicts in his relationships.

3. Door:

   (a) Door: gives indications pertaining to the artist's open feelings about inviting others into his life or his environment.

   (b) Open: strong need to receive warmth from the external world.

   (c) With lock or hinges: defensiveness.

   (d) Without doorknob: undemonstrative, distant, reserved, aloof; hard to get to know; others have to work hard to get into their hearts and their environments.

4. Fence around house:
   Need for emotional protection, territorial.

5. Shutters:

   (a) Closed: defensiveness and possibly withdrawal.

   (b) Open: ability to easily make interpersonal adjustments; fits in with most crowds.

6. Walkway:

   (a) Inviting: says "Welcome!"

   (b) Very long-open to others, but feels of need to know others before letting them into his life or environment.

   (c) Narrow at house, broad at end: superficially friendly.

7. Windows:

   (a) Absence of window: withdrawn.

   (b) Bars across window: uneasiness or discomfort about something.

   (c) Bare: direct, to-the-point.

   (d) Curtains: feminine quality associated with gaiety, a need to make things right and perfectionism.

The tree

The drawing of the tree is believed to be associated with one's life role and one's ego. Tree drawings have been considered especially rich in providing insights concerning the artist's "life content," and reflects his long-standing, unconscious feelings towards himself.

The following signs or marks that might appear on a tree drawing are just a tiny sample of possible interpretations for exploring emotional feelings related to the examinee.

1. Extremely large tree with solid trunk: artist feels a sense of responsibility about sheltering and protecting his whole family.

2. Tiny tree with faint, sparse branches: ego of the artist is somewhat fragile and he may possibly have emotional needs that are unmet.

The person

1. Person: represents the actual creator of the picture.

2. Placement:

    (a) Distant, away from house: indicates that the artist does not feel a great deal of closeness to the people in the home.

    (b) Directly next to the house: artist feels harmonious, loving and very close to the people inside.

3. Specifics:

    (a) Tiny: creator tends to sell himself short, lacks self-confidence and does not realize all of his personal attributes.

    (b) Any feature that is indiscernible: be it mouth or ears; the artist tends to have a problem in that area. Mouth imperfections are typically associated with trouble communicating, ear flaws may indicate a hearing problem.

    (c) Overemphasized or intentionally omitted features indicate areas that the artist finds particularly unattractive about himself.

    (d) Artists who draw profiles to represent themselves, seldom look at life directly in the face and have a tendency to not confront problems head-on.

    (e) A considerably large head drawn in relation to the remainder of the body symbolizes high intellectual skills.

COMPREHENDING THE SYMBOLIC LANGUAGE OF DOODLES

Doodles are as unique to each person as handwriting. The difference is that we are all taught to write, but no one is taught to doodle. That's why doodles offer an uncensored look into a deeper part of our personalities, our inherent desires, drives and impulses.

Only about two thirds of the population admit to being doodlers; the rest insist they never doodle. Saying "I don't doodle" is like saying "I don't dream." Both dreaming and doodling are activities we are often unaware of doing. Sometimes the paper ends up in the trash without ever being noticed; but even if you just underline or circle words, you're a doodler.

Doodling is often a way of relieving stress. The repetition of lines and shapes helps a person relax and focus his thoughts on the problem at hand. Today modern psychotherapists rely on doodles to help them understand a client's subconscious feelings.

When individuals are drawing freely and without direction, they are expressing an intimate part of their own personality and perceptions. The experience becomes a time for independent thought and action and allows the individual to release his own feelings and attitudes.

The usual directive given to individuals when using this technique is a request to "draw anything" and to "verbalize whatever thoughts and feelings" they might be experiencing. Free drawing increases the opportunity for persons being evaluated to open up and enhances the possibility to demonstrate impulsive actions, reveal fantasies, or provide freer associations to areas of internal conflict.

You are what you doodle or you doodle what you are. Your doodles, or aimless squiggles, are fugitives of the subconscious and paint a picture of your inner thoughts.

Squiggles, squares, triangles, or arrows flow into your consciousness via your pen or pencil. They generally happen when you are on the telephone, at a meeting, or when you are bored. In other words, when your mind wanders, so does your pen. If you concentrate on what you are doodling, you are drawing and drawings do not tap the unconscious in the same way.

Although doodles paint a picture of your inner thoughts, they must be repeated at least six times to be considered as part of your personal expression. These subconscious markings may serve as an outlet for emotions and also show creative abilities such as artistic flair or musical talent. Doodles provide definite clues as to how people see themselves and because they are unique as the personalities who make them, doodles should not be written off lightly. They are often a release for something you wish, but are never quite capable of verbally expressing.

What Your Doodles Reveal

Dollar signs are common to the dealer or gambler in a casino or someone preoccupied with the idea of winning money.

Squares indicate the logical ability to solve problems. When they are connected, it indicates that the writer has the ability to build one thought upon another. This type of writer is an aggressive, purposeful type who likes structure and discipline.

Triangular-shaped drawings indicate that the writer is judgmental, well organized, rational and intelligent. Upward-pointed triangles indicate someone who is a high achiever who needs to keep moving and downward-pointing triangles show a more passive, less ambitious person.

A tic-tac-toe diagram depicts a writer who is competitive and places a great deal of importance on winning.

Stars indicate a writer exploring his creativity.

A musical clef or wavy lines depicts rhythm. There is a strong indication here of someone who enjoys music and dancing.

Hearts drawn disclose a writer who is filled with compassion, understanding, and love. Hearts pierced by arrows show a wish for passion and love. A broken heart means exactly that.

Faces (especially smiling ones) reveal a writer who likes to communicate and who enjoys relationships. It also represents the personality the writer shows to the world. If the features are faintly drawn, the writer tends to be withdrawn and feels self-conscious in social situations. When features are dark or overemphasized, the writer may be domineering, but feel inadequate.

Profiles only, displays a writer who never looks life in the face. He always seems to come from the side. If there is any feature that is distorted in the drawing, it indicates that the writer has a problem in that area.

The house depicts one's family life. The more features and details, the more involved the "doodler" is with his family.

Flowers, when doodled repeatedly, reveal a person who has a love of beauty and may be searching for love. Small buds show potential for growth; fully opened flowers disclose a writer who is highly developed. A rose suggests someone who is looking for perfection and the mystery of life; but its thorns stand for pain and the wounds of love. Flowers also proclaim a person who is affectionate, caring and who likes to interact with others.

A boat drawn on a calm sea suggests security; a boat in a storm indicates some anxiety over relationships.

Kathy

When a person doodles someone's name, it means that he is curious or concerned about that person. The style in which the name is drawn (big, small, heavy or light) provides clues to the writer's feelings. Teenagers commonly make designs around their names as they search for their identities.

Rain drawn may be a sign of depression, especially when it contains many rain-drops. Dark clouds reveal a person who may feel he is in a stormy environment.

Calm water demonstrates a contemplative, peaceful mood; stormy seas indicate that the writer is worried. Figures floating in water may be a sign of depression; any-thing drawn under water suggests anger or helplessness.

Moons represent intuition, romance and passion. A crescent moon shows eagerness for new developments. Doodled with a crescent facing right, the moon indicates a writer whose goals are in sight; to the left, the writer should reevaluate his goals.

Upward arrows are signs of a person who is ambitious and optimistic.

Downward arrows are indicators of pes-simism, and the idea that the writer is a bit of a downer.

Horizontal arrows are signs of indecisiveness and indicate a person who straddles the fence.

Doodles and spirals that increase in size depict a writer who continuously wants the upper hand in a situation. Spirals are universal signs depicting concern with expansion and continuity—two of the dynamic aspects of life. This may also depict a tinge of self-deception.

Eyes doodled consistently are a sign that the writer is suspicious.

Three little pigs (or perhaps other objects) is a sign that the writer desires togetherness. The sizes depict belonging and a desire for family unity.

Animals reflect the self-concept of the writer. Domestic animals reveal a "tame" personality. Very small creatures (such as bugs or mice) disclose a fear or phobia, whereas jungle beasts show aggression. A giraffe, though, is a favorite of those who are exploring their sexuality. The longer the neck, the more the writer wants to explore!

Squiggles indicate that the writer is very enthusiastic, imaginative, independent, energetic and a free spirit.

Up-and-down lines disclose someone who has an insatiable curiosity and a desire to learn. It is an indicator that the writer is constantly trying to improve himself.

Loops and the l-like structure displays fluidity and grace. If the loops are large and widely spaced, they indicate a person who has a great deal of imagination. If the loops are small and/or tightly spaced, the writer may be a bit wound up.

Circles symbolize reality, love and playfulness. If the circles are filled with designs, shapes or faces, they reveal a person who is interesting, creative and filled with ideas.

Chains divulge unity and bonding. If the chain is unbroken, the writer is feeling "together," but somewhat restricted. If the chain is broken, the writer indicates a need to break free.

Vertical jagged lines proclaim a person who is feeling quite edgy and/or angry. If they are doodled around another form, the writer is looking for revenge. If doodled inside another form, the writer is trying to contain his anger.

How to Make Sense of Your Doodles

1. **Pencil pressure.** Heavy pressure usually indicates tension. Light pressure or erasures can be signs of a hesitant, indecisive, shy person, or someone who is flexible and adaptable.

2. **Types of lines or strokes.** Horizontal lines are favored by more introverted people, vertical lines suggest a more assertive personality. Lots of curves and circular shapes may mean the doodler is an accepting person, while straight or rigid lines suggest a straight, rigid and probably stubborn person.

3.   **Size.** Unusually large doodles that take up an entire page are typically done by "show-offs" who may have a large inferiority complex. Usually, small doodles scrunched into a corner of the paper mean that the doodler is depressed or feels inadequate.

4.   **Placement.** The average doodler may totally cover the page. The optimist with high hopes and dreams, generally doodles high up on the paper. A pessimistic, dependent doodler often draws low on the page or uses the bottom edge of the paper. Doodles done only on the left edge may mean a preoccupation with the past, whereas doodling on the right edge can show a person who is looking toward the future. Doodling in the absolute center of the page reveals a rigid personality.

5.   **Numbers.** The number of objects that are doodled at one time is frequently of personal significance. It may denote the "doodler's" number of family members.

Results Of: "The Get-To-Know-Yourself Quiz"

Circle: Represents wholeness, a need for independence and the space to develop your own identity.

Cross or Plus Sign: Symbolizes relationships, integration and the need for connection.

Spiral: Represents growth, evolution, the need for change.

Triangle: Symbolizes goals and dreams. Identifying, pursuing and attaining a goal is very important.

Square: Suggests stability and security. The need to build something based on a strong foundation and to seek consistency and completion in these efforts.

Next:	Consider the meaning of the position you chose for each symbol.
Position 1:	Where you think you are or where you might like to be.
Position 2:	Your strengths at the moment.
Position 3:	The (possibly unconscious) growth process on which you are working.
Position 4:	Your motivation for change.
Position 5:	A process you have outgrown or are resisting.

A PERSONAL NOTE. . .ALICE

A child's drawing is so telling. When my neighbor's son Bruce was a young child, he enjoyed visiting with me because of the many puzzles I would give him to solve. On one particular day, though, I asked him to draw a picture for me. I suggested he draw his house, a tree and a portrait of himself waiting for the school bus.

The picture was detailed and surprisingly good. His house sported a chimney with smoke blowing from it indicating the warmth and love inside, but one disturbing feature caught my eye. The third-floor window had black, heavy bars drawn across it.

I asked his mother if there was anything unusual going on at home and she replied, "Not really." She did mention, though, that she had moved Bruce to an upstairs bedroom so that he would have his own room, but evidently he had not yet adjusted to the move because each morning she found him downstairs in his old bedroom that he shared with his brother.

I am happy to note that after Bruce was moved back into his old room, the burglar bars in his drawing disappeared.

What better story to relate concerning a doodle than the story of my relationship with Jan Hargrave. Jan and I met five years ago and liked each other immediately. Little did we know that our paths would meet again in such a meaningful way; hence, this book.

While proofreading and discussing our mutual project, Jan confided that she had observed my body language and my level of confidence at our original meeting and knew instantly that she wanted to work on a future project with me. Jan assured me that she had information to share and thought that our collaboration would be a unique endeavor.

I began to smile and said, "I know." I told her that I remembered vividly her "telling doodles." She seemed rather surprised, but pleased and flattered when she asked "What doodles?" I said, "Your daisy flower drawings." What she didn't realize was that when I looked at her drawings of endless rows of three daisy flowers, I saw her willingness to share, the strength of her organizational ability and her high level of integrity. Also, since neither of the daisies in her drawings overshadowed the others, I knew that she didn't have to always be in charge to get a job done. The flowers depicted gaiety and merriment, two traits that I cherish, thus making my friend and I bound for life.

Unmasking the Face

The human face is the
Masterpiece of God
The eyes reveal the soul,
The mouth the flesh.
The chin stands for purpose,
The nose means will.
But over and behind all,
Is that fleeting something,
We call "Expression."

Elbert Hubbard, 1800

IT'S ALL IN THE FACE

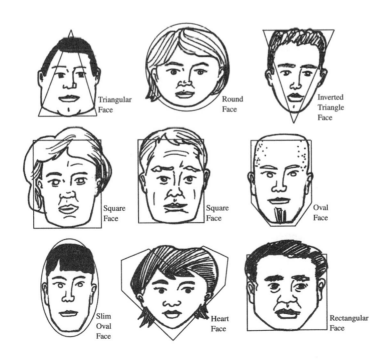

Triangular Face

Round Face

Inverted Triangle Face

Square Face

Square Face

Oval Face

Slim Oval Face

Heart Face

Rectangular Face

We read faces, we cannot avoid it. It's both an ancient art and a modern science. We have long heard the commonly known expressions of: *tight lipped, conehead, face-to-face selling, saving face* or *highbrow* that seem to associate facial features with behavior. We can learn a good deal about the people in our lives through their faces. Those who master the art of interpreting facial features can gain a deeper knowledge of the people they meet. Everything is written in the face; one has only to summon the determination—and the courage to have a good look at these signs. Understanding face reading allows one to form more meaningful and more satisfactory relationships with friends, colleagues and partners.

How often have you taken one look at someone and "known" that he was not to be trusted? Or on the other hand, how often have you instantly been sure that some new acquaintance was someone who was going to be your friend? You "know" because you can instinctively see his character in his face. In activities as diverse as jury selection, selling face-to-face and resolving family problems, faces are spelling out vital information. It is all in the face; even cartoonists and casting directors for film and theater strive to select faces that convince us of the characters portrayed.

Our longing to discover something about our own destiny is as old as humanity itself. *Siang Mien*, the art of reading faces, goes back more than 3,000 years, and has been kept secret, passed down through the generations from master to pupil. Books about the interpretation of faces existed from the earliest times but were only accessible to the Chinese emperors and were guarded as treasures.

Just how much a ruler was influenced by the art of reading faces is shown, for example, by the Emperor Tsin-Che-Wong, who ruled the Middle Kingdom in 221BC. This power-mad leader ordered all the literature in his kingdom to be burned—part of which consisted the priceless writings from the time of Confucius, including books on reading faces. He did this in the belief that these writings would expose him as an evil and treacherous tyrant. Fear of the discovery of his true character went so deep that he flatly refused to let his court painter portray him as he was, even though the custom of the time demanded it. He ordered a completely different portrait to be painted—with a face showing favorable features that he presumed would convince his subjects of his goodness and kindness.

Much of what is known about *Siang Mien* today has been handed down orally. This age-old wisdom, though, has prevailed and flourishes through the knowledge of *Siang Mien* masters who travel the world. The serious study of faces and their relationship to personality originated independently in China, and then in Greece with ancient Greeks such as Pythagoras and Aristotle. In the Roman Empire it became a respected profession, and in England during the reign of Elizabeth I, it was considered a threat to the authorities.

In the twentieth century three men changed it to a modern science. Edward Vincent Jones, a California judge, categorically linked facial features and character traits. Robert Whiteside, who coined the term "Personalogy," worked on statistically validating these linkages, and was subsequently joined by William Burtis. They continued the testing and correlation of over 70 facial features and behavior traits, but it was Judge Jones who put the subject on a modern footing. Since he had many opportunities to study the physical features and the behavior of defendants, witnesses and attorneys for the prosecution and the defense, he recorded facial features and the characteristics that accompanied them. As his amount of data accumulated, Jones saw that there were clear-cut trends. Together with Robert Whiteside and William Burtis, Judge Jones conducted a study pertaining to the relationship of facial features to behavior traits of 1050 adults. Measurements of 67 facial features were recorded and correlated with personality factors using standard statistical techniques. The analysis of the results showed an impressive 92 percent accuracy per trait.

Corporations recognize the need for people to understand each other better before they can work together effectively. Written tests are used to categorize psychological and personality traits and workshops are conducted to help employees study each other's behavior. Later, placards on employee desks announce to their peers such personal styles as *expressive, amiable, analytical, etc.* This may seem extreme to anyone who has not been involved in the process, however, it does show the importance people attach to understanding each other quickly before working together.

Written tests are fine for corporations; however, the rest of us need something which gives similar results without written tests or lengthy behavior study. Face reading can provide critical information quickly.

FACE SHAPES, IN GENERAL

Many faces can be classified at a glance, as certain typical shapes: round, oval, rectangular, square, angular or triangular. The art of reading faces consists in taking all the features combined in the face as well as the shape of the face, the complexion and the bone structure. Generally, a broad face reveals a high ego and an elevated level of confidence, whereas a narrow face discloses a person not sure of himself, somewhat lacking in ego. A distinctive bony structure to the face indicates that this person can behave harshly and ruthlessly both to himself and to others and that in his philosophy of life, there is very little room for bubbling over with *joie de vivre* or other spontaneous cheerfulness.

Full-faced individuals like an easy life, crave comforts and pleasures of all kinds, and tend to have a bias for sweet things. This type of person is extremely amusing to be with—so long as he is the center of attention. If he feels he is being edged out, he regards this as disrespectful and appears insulted. These optimists would find it unthinkable to reveal their frustration to anybody; they would rather swallow it and put on an incredibly charming smile.

According to the Chinese art of interpretation, the color of the complexion serves as a barometer, allowing us to read a person's immediate state of health and general disposition. People with rosy facial skin that is well supplied with blood, automatically radiate a positive approach to life. The character of such a person is affectionate, sometimes even romantic. They are extremely easy-going and will generally try to find a reasonable compromise to avoid quarrels. By nature they are highly intelligent, and go to endless adversity and effort to further their knowledge.

At first glance, a reddish complexion tells us that a person either gets out of breath after any exertion or possibly suffers from high blood pressure. In reading a face, though, we must be tactful when investigating the reasons for redness of the complexion. Some very active, energetic people easily change face color when they are extremely anxious. Reddish-complexion people love their independence and can become impatient and unfriendly if someone gets too close to them. Their ruddy complexion leads one to assume that they enjoy being out in the open and that physical exercise has a settling effect on their nervous energy.

A darker, but frequently pasty, complexion is usually associated with someone with a pessimistic attitude. People of this skin type frequently take life too seriously. Their intelligence does not allow them to take things as they are; instead they will brood over problems night after night. It is typical of this type to flit from one subject or field of work to the next. Nothing bores them more than routine.

Round-Shaped Face

People with extremely round faces can expect harmony and happiness in the family from middle age onwards. They are born hosts, good entertainers and considered to be pack rats. Lots of children and a large, extended family guarantee that they will be cared for and respected in their old age. People with round faces often give the impression of lethargy, passivity and find much satisfaction in eating and socializing.

People with round-shaped faces are skilled in dealing with others and their pleasant manner makes them born diplomats. They are particularly clever and never regard serious problems as the end of the world. At work they are considered smart and quick, but they tend to be careless and frequently forget to look after their own interests because they are too busy to think about them. In private, round-faced people enjoy the single life and most do not get married until they are in their forties. They make wonderful, warm, caring parents and end up having many children.

Square-Shaped Face

Siang Mien recognizes two types of square-shaped faces. The type seen most frequently is a short face with very full cheeks. Those with the long square type of face are usually tall, often over six feet. The personality trait that is immediately recognizable in most people of this face shape is their sympathetic aura. People of this type understand better than anyone how to disguise their feelings by appearing severe. They have a definite predisposition to solitariness—unless they find someone of exactly the same mind.

People with square-shaped faces maintain a pronounced sense of justice and will defend with great passion what they believe to be right. They love surprises, have a delightful sense of humor and are highly intelligent. Fate seems to take a hand in the way these people fall on their feet time and again—either because they suddenly excel as the head of a company or because they accumulate financial riches quite unexpectedly. A leaning towards politics or law is also typical; an above-average number of this face shape can be found on the judge's bench or in parliament.

In private, both males and females with square-shaped faces cherish the more exquisite pleasures of life. If they see an object they desire, they display unbelievable energy and imagination to get it. Once they do, however, they will go off in search of new attractions. Since they tire of things easily, this type of person may get married several times in his lifetime.

Heart-Shaped Face

The heart-shaped face is very expressive and elegantly proportioned. It is the most common for the female face. Women with heart-shaped faces have a mysterious aura and appear very attractive. They are always aware of their image, beauty and aesthetic sense.

People with heart-shaped faces—not just women, but men as well—possess an enormous determination to succeed. They maintain a very optimistic attitude toward life and are exceptionally quick to display their enthusiasm. Women with heart-shaped faces frequently rise to the highest social levels through their determined efforts to achieve success, and because of this, they are often unfairly condemned and described as arrogant and unscrupulous.

Men with heart-shaped faces often have a tendency toward chauvinism. They show a profound dislike for routine and always seek occupations that are stimulating and intriguing. In relationships, they make as high demands of their partners as they do of themselves.

Inverted Triangle-Shaped Face

The inverted triangle-shaped face is marked by a broad forehead and pronounced eye area. These people are career and material oriented and possess loads of energy. They spend virtually their whole life in the pursuit of knowledge. People with inverted triangle-shaped faces experience periods of melancholy which dramatically reduces their achievements. One should, however, be wary of trying to cheer them up and of trying to make them snap out of this negative mood—it will not work.

Getting close to them and winning their trust can be a lengthy undertaking. Although they have many friends, this type of person often feels basically alone. Their original and imaginative character is particularly successful in occupations where they can be the center of attention. They adore careers on stage or in the theatre.

People with this face shape fall deeply and passionately in love. They feel that their lives would not be complete without physical love, but often, they cannot distinguish real feelings from a passing fancy.

Slim, Oval-Shaped Face

A person with a slim, oval-shaped face has a broad forehead, high cheek bones and a small pointed chin. Their intelligence is outstanding and impressive. They are extremely talented and constantly bubble over with ideas, but must work hard to succeed.

In spite of their many positive tendencies, they always make friends with the wrong people because they readily allow themselves to be dazzled by outward appearances where feelings are concerned. More serious, though, is their tendency to shameless exaggeration. They often get so carried away by their own dramatics that they can hardly distinguish between appearance and reality. They continuously strive for power and generally map out their careers early in their youth.

People with this face shape rarely have problems revealing their feelings and desires when they are in love. They may scare off their lovers time after time, though, because they are so suspicious and often have problems trusting others.

Oval-Shaped Face

The perfect oval-shaped face, also known as the King face, is angular in structure with forehead, cheeks, and jawline strongly defined. This type of face is commonly thought of as being the aesthetic ideal since its features are in exact symmetry.

People with perfect oval-shaped faces exert an almost magical force of attraction over other people. Thanks to their spontaneity and capacity for enthusiasm, they give the impression that they know how to have a great time. The fact, though, is that real friendship often remains an unfulfilled dream for them.

At work, the natural authority of people with this face shape makes it easy for them to assume positions of leadership. The possibility that they might not succeed seems totally foreign to them. If they feel that their work is not being sufficiently appreciated, especially financially, they quickly decide to throw it all in without warning.

An individual with a perfect oval-shaped face is considered to be the ideal passionate partner, but it is unlikely that a relationship with this type of person will lead to the registry office. These individuals usually try to find partners who manage to worship them in the manner that they feel they deserve.

Triangular-Shaped Face

The triangular-shaped face is distinguished by the expressive musculature of the face. Although the forehead is relatively narrow, the chin area is broad and angular and the cheek bones are pronounced.

People with triangular-shaped faces tend to be bossy and self-centered. A more positive aspect of their character is their round-the-clock commitment to their beliefs. They possess an intense desire to acquire a good reputation through being financially secure.

Their relationship with their partners can be described as highly explosive. Disagreements are the order of the day. They only remain bearable if the partner accepts quietly all their decisions. But, if two triangular face shaped individuals fall in love, they can change the world. They take infinite pains over their mutual promotion—and presumably also manage to bring it about.

People with this face shape possess a severe need to be respected and valued for their achievements. Their aggressiveness knows no bounds and is directed at one and all. They are rarely found socializing—not just because they prefer to be alone, but because it is contrary to their nature to be at the center of things or to gossip about trivialities.

These individuals will only enter into a relationship if it promises them guaranteed financial prosperity, however unromantic that may sound. Their constant striving for power and for a life free from worry needs to be advocated by their partner. If this type knows he has someone standing behind him, he will do his utmost to safeguard the happiness of his private life and that of his children.

Rectangular-Shaped Face

In the rectangular-shaped face, the distance from the forehead to the chin is extremely short, and the face is wide and stocky. This type of person is down to earth and can work hard when he needs to. Typically this person lacks the ability to put existing ideas into practice. Perhaps this is due to his inclination to search continually for the ultimate proof of his ability. One should refrain as much as possible from criticizing this type of person—he detests it and there is not a shred of evidence to suggest that he will benefit from such criticism.

People with this face shape have absolutely no use for authority, either exerting it or putting up with it. They possess a fairly fickle nature, have excessive creative abilities, and could possibly cause a sensation as a media star, or at least become reasonably well-known.

They have a difficult time expressing themselves and have a tendency to bitterly throw their admiration to a new lover, rather than salvage an existing relationship. Those who want to cope with this type of individual will have to face the fact that their love life will be rather conservative and that their erotic dreams may well be smashed to pieces.

Asymmetrical-Shaped Face and Features

Facial features as well as the shape of the face are important. Most people have several asymmetrical facial features, that is, their features are not exactly even on both sides of their face. An eye slightly higher than the other, an ear a tad bit lower than the other or an irregularly-formed nose, for example, are very common. One rarely comes across total uniformity when observing faces. Either one half of the face is longer and/or broader than the other, the mouth is slightly lopsided, or some other characteristic is irregular.

The stronger the difference between the two sides of the face, the greater are the mood swings the person with asymmetrical facial features experiences. Excessive asymmetrical facial features on children result from parents being significantly different from each other in their appearance. Some people may, in fact, feel as though they experience dual personalities because of the push and pull of the different traits.

These people are masters of all the tricks needed to use others for their own ends and can be intensely unforgiving if anyone thinks they are being unfair. A certain amount of stress and action will not hurt the person with this type of face; he knows how to channel his generous supply of physical energy in the right direction. One should avoid over-loading them with too much responsibility or tying them down too hard. They will use their disarming charm to extricate themselves and leave it to others to make their mistakes right.

People with asymmetrical features have a highly developed emotional life and can be incredibly considerate, affectionate and easy-going, even if they themselves get a raw deal. It is apparent from the way they throw themselves into amorous adventures that love is their favorite hobby. A relationship quickly becomes the focal point of their life. As does the next one, and the next one.

HAIR—PHYSICAL INSULATION

The finer the hair the more sensitive the person is to smell, sound, taste, and elegance versus roughness. An individual with fine hair prefers quality rather than quantity and gets his feelings hurt easily and quickly. People with thicker hair follicles are less sensitive to pain. They like things on the grand scale, as in sound, amounts of food, and hearty laughter. It takes longer to get under their skin, and they appear insensitive to other people's needs. People with medium thickness hair are able to adapt easily to what is around them and are able to give and take without much problem.

FOREHEAD—THOUGHTS AND INTELLIGENCE

If the forehead is broad, it is assumed that a correspondingly broad spectrum of knowledge is concealed behind it. The forehead represents an individual's intellectual faculties, aspirations and resources. A person with a broad forehead has no qualms about speaking up and is quick to take on any intellectual challenge. He stands up for his own rights, possess outstanding rhetorical skills and talents and can sometimes become extremely unreasonable when his beliefs are not accepted. A narrowing forehead indicates narrow-mindedness and pessimism. These individuals tend to have little confidence in themselves and their judgment and are thought to be not as precise as those with wider foreheads. It is as though their intellectual and emotional properties are muddled together. A ledge across the lower forehead is indicative of a person who is very systematic, highly observant and sees things as the right way, the wrong way and his way.

Forehead Facial Lines

After a while, certain patterns of lines develop in the face from repetitious expression of one kind or another. It is as if remnants of certain feelings have been permanently etched in the face by redundancy of expression. G. Orwell in "Closing Words," noted that "At 50, everyone has the face he deserves." Since the eyes and eyebrows are so much a part of emotional expression, the forehead, which is affected by their movement, records habitual affective patterns. Specific emotions write their story on the individual's forehead.

A permanently wrinkled forehead means that the individual is emotionally expressive. While no particular feelings can be read from these horizontal grooves, the forehead that frequently pulls down into a frown creating a distinctive pattern of vertical lines, on the other hand, reveals a long experience with worry and tension.

A person with parallel bars or worry lines down the center of his forehead has a high need to be correct. Much of his time is spent worrying about how to prevent mistakes. He does not like to be wrong. A person with engraved vertical lines is exacting by nature and strives to be certain before acting. This is the individual who will agonize over a decision for fear of failure. He will toss alternatives back and forth and double-think his conclusions. Therefore, if an attorney needs someone to inject doubt into the deliberations, he should retain the professional worrier with vertical forehead indentations on his jury.

The worrier is frequently a good candidate to become the holdout on a criminal case. Such a person worries constantly about making the right decision and is hard to convince that any given decision is the correct one. A worrier generally feels more comfortable and safe *not* deciding. The worrier can hold decisions in limbo indefinitely.

The intelligent individual with worry lines is even more significant in jury dynamics. He can back up his doubts with persuasive counterarguments that can throw deliberations into a stall. Long after others are convinced that damages should be awarded, this person is still uncertain.

FACE WIDTH—SELF CONFIDENCE

Elevated self-confidence is seen by the width of the face at the vertical ledge or bone which is located at the outer edge of both eyebrows. The width of the face at this outer edge is compared with the length of the face. People with high self confidence enjoy a challenge, are assertive, highly motivated, positive and focus on results rather than difficulties. You can spot them right away when you walk into a meeting—they look in charge. People with narrower faces are the support people in a group and may not necessarily be comfortable in a leadership situation. They are much more aware of their limitations, eager to please, fear rejection and stay with what is familiar until they have enough knowledge to take major steps forward.

Round face:	Optimistic, diplomatic, caring
Square face:	Stubborn, opinionated, domineering

Round with soft features:	Gentle, soft, peaceful, yielding
Heart face:	Mysterious, determined, enthusiastic
Inverted-triangular face:	Sensitive to criticism, emotionally responsive, dreamer, passionate
Slim-oval face:	Intelligent, manipulative, dramatic
Perfect-oval face:	Spontaneous, authoritative, attractive
Triangular face:	Materialistic, self-centered, explosive
Rectangular face:	Down-to-earth, passive, fickle

JAW LINE—AUTHORITATIVE

The authoritative trait is expressed by the width of the jaw line in comparison to the width of the self-confidence line (outside of eyebrow area). When the jaw line is wider than the self-confidence line, the authoritativeness trait is high. As the jaw becomes narrower than the self-confidence line, the authoritative trait is less pronounced and the person appears weaker. An individual with this trait takes direction well, but does not like it.

The appearance of authority and of being in command of the situation is indicated by the wide jaw. The firm, angular jaw is a sign of defiance, stubbornness and of a person who means what he says. He gains respect from others because of his decisive tone and total lack of doubt. People with this trait may be annoying to some because they appear as "know-it-alls" when their behavior is not in check. The softer, rounded jaw reveals a personality that is gentler and more forgiving. People with jaw lines that are equal with the eye-width area are comfortable in positions of authority, or in merely taking directions.

LIPS AND MOUTH—FEELINGS, LOVE, HEALTH

As a general rule, the upper lip represents feelings, passive needs, words, and the lower lip represents action and the active expression of individual desires. In addition, the color and appearance of the lips are equally important. Delicately radiant lips are a sign of health and well-being, whereas if they are dull, it signifies that the body is out of balance, and perhaps organic changes are taking place.

If the lips are a light pink color, it is thought that the individual will be quite modest in his demands and needs. If the lips are red and obviously well supplied with blood, the person is seen as honest and direct, but also quite ambitious. Dark lips indicate a materialistic person who consciously controls his feelings and appears never to lose control.

The most noticeable distinction when observing lips is that of size: full lips versus tight lips. Tight-lippers are characteristically stingy, cold, businesslike, efficient, punctual, rigid, hard-nosed and verbally concise. The steel-willed determination of these individuals is certainly reflected in the meaningful British expression "keep a stiff upper lip." Conducting a conversation with this type of person about his family might wind up in a monologue, since he does not like to waste time on irrelevant details. Full-lipped people, on the other hand, enjoy talking about their family members, and are inclined to be warm, kind, soft, affectionate, generous and compassionate.

Lip reading for thinness or thickness, in combination with other body language cues, is a diagnostic aid during jury selection. Generally speaking, tight-lipped people with beady eyes and taut facial skin are bad for plaintiffs. Even if they award money, it is a driblet. They believe pain should be endured and their frugal ways will not allow them to give away money for a misfortune that could have been overcome with determination and grit. Plaintiff's attorneys should have a strike ready for veniremen with skinny lips. Jurors keeping a stiff upper lip will expect the complainant to do the same.

People who have kept their lips loose for most of their lives usually make good plaintiff's jurors, especially if they are wide-eyed and plump. They will want to take care of the poor plaintiff the same way they handle their own pain—with indulgence. Their desire to soothe the injured party can distort their logic. The defense attorney would be wise to strike these sentimental people off his list, but the plaintiff's counsel should simply smile and go on.

In using lip size as an aid to diagnosing potential jurors, it is best to assume that lips are formed through emotional development. As in the case of speakers or entertainers, lip size can be developmentally produced by repeated use of certain muscles around the mouth.

Small lips: People with small lips are strong-willed and charming. They do not allow difficulties to get them down, have a strong yearning for independence and are quite bossy.

Large, full mouth: These people are extremely outgoing. They are dependent on the constant admiration of others and tend to have a hard time at developing serious relationships. They are extremely generous with time and money, quite impulsive, excessive talkers and can be relied on to be faithfully passionate.

Upper lip thicker than lower lip: The Chinese regard this as a sign of insincerity, however in Western culture, these people are judged much more positively. They are emotional and generous to themselves and others. They are also considered to be skillful speakers who can plead a cause convincingly and well. Most of them have a weakness for good food and are often wonderful cooks. They enjoy poetry and other arts and appear to take love lightly.

Lower lip thicker than upper lip: People with a thicker lower lip have a tendency to be very talkative. They are quick-witted and have a very good chance in the field of entertainment; they enjoy amusing other people. A person with a thick lower lip appears very sensual and attractive and seems to give the impression that he is searching compulsively for love.

Thin upper and thin lower lip: The "tight-lipped" phrase fits this type. They tend to be stingy with their time and words and will not tell you everything about themselves, their feelings or the situation. They are concise, to the point, and do not like their time wasted. They sometimes are viewed as using and abusing of other people's generosity.

Teeth angle in: Closemouthed and reserved. They tend to hold back verbally and are very secretive about personal matters.

Teeth angle out: Verbose and gabby. They possess an intense desire to talk, even about personal problems, and appear very friendly.

UNDERSTANDING THE EXPRESSIONS OF EMOTIONS IN THE EYES, EYEBROWS, NOSE AND FACIAL LINES

Skin

Soft, loose skin:	Indecisive, yielding, low energy.
Firm skin:	Vigorous, direct, decisive.

Eyes

Close together:	Low tolerance, perfectionist, accepts people's problems, wants to change the world, is hard to please.
Widely spaced:	High tolerance, fair, just, even-tempered, not concerned about details, live and let live attitude, will bend rules if necessary.
Equally spaced:	Fair, even-tempered.
Large eyes:	Emotional, thinks with heart rather than head, easily hurt, sentimental.
Small eyes:	Lack of emotion. Matter of fact nature, self-centered, tough minded.
Glassy-eyed:	Elsewhere. Mind is not with the moment. Under pressure. Tendency to make the poor decisions.
Eyes slanted downward:	Critical of others. Will notice flaws quickly.
Eyes slanted upward:	Not very critical of others. Easy to get along with.
Inner eyes level with each other:	Conventional judgment, judges based on facts.
One inner eye higher than the other:	Unconventional judgment, judges by mood or feeling.

Eyebrows

Flat eyebrows:	Harmony, strives for unity, great team player.
Arched eyebrows:	Dramatic ability, good sense of timing, discriminating.
New moon shaped eyebrows:	Reflects balance and equality. Leads a carefree, laid back lifestyle.
Close set eyebrows:	Spontaneous personality that is inclined to explosiveness.
Eyebrows close to eye:	Friendly, informal, down to earth. What you see is what you get.
Eyebrows high above eye:	Aloof, demands respect, reserved, hidden innerself, selective.
Thin eyebrows:	Disciplined, orderly.
Thick eyebrows:	Generous, very emotional.
Lots of eyelid visible:	Direct actionist, doer, makes things happen, often leaps before he looks.
No eyelid visible:	Analytical, wants to know details, logical. Delays making a decision until all facts are known.
Above eyebrow protuberances:	Concerned with detail. Exacting by nature, very observant.

Nose

Concave nose:	Helper, careless with money. Will work hard for a pat on the back.
Straight, or Roman nose:	Money conscious. Expects to be paid for his efforts.
Hook nose:	Good business sense, knows the value of a dollar, very capable of making money, is extremely price oriented.

Narrow nostrils:	Low self reliance.
Flared nostrils:	High self reliance.

Lines

Lines between eye-brows:	Worrier, perfectionist, demanding.
No lines between eye-brows:	No time consciousness. Live and let live nature.
Lines from nose to side of mouth:	Self expression lines. Articulate, passionate. The deeper the lines, the more expressive the person.
Crows feet:	Humor lines. Is easily amused. Enjoys laughter. (These cannot be rubbed out with cream.)
Extended crows feet down around the cheek:	Rhetoric lines. Likes elegant phrases. (Seen on politicians, speakers, actors.)
Thick skin:	High physical insulation. Outdoor type that can take roughness.
Thin skinned:	Delicate, gentleness, low physical insulation.
Cosmetic changes:	Concerned with appearance, aesthetic beauty.

FACE READING IN PRACTICE

The most fascinating thing about the human face is that each one is different. Although amazing similarities can be detected in different people, no two people will ever have exactly identical faces.

Even identical twins do not have precisely the same face. In the special case of twins, there are the tiniest of differences, perhaps in the expression of the eyes, in the smile, in the texture of the skin, or a hair line which does not follow precisely the same course.

How often do children hear family and friends say, "You look just like your mother." Or, "You are the spitting image of your father." "You write exactly like your mother does." Here "looking exactly" and "writing exactly" simply means being similar and possessing resembling characteristics. Each individual face can be interpreted. To be an expert face reader one must learn to be a meticulously keen observer and to pay precise attention to microscopic details, even if they seem unimportant at first sight.

Also, while reading faces, we should not forget that stress, tenseness of any kind and alcohol can give a false impression of a face. The result of these three factors is misleading and can distort true emotions.

The simplest thing to do is to begin by using your own face as a "test object." Decode your features, and then with the knowledge you have obtained, try to find a parallel with your character traits (which you probably know best) and your behavior. In this way you will learn, with a little practice, how to combine the interpretations of the individual parts of the face, little by little into a homogeneous picture.

Check for yourself just how familiar you now are with the secrets of reading faces. Some face-reading tests have been provided. Give it a try. *FACE IT, YOU HAVE NOTHING TO LOSE!*

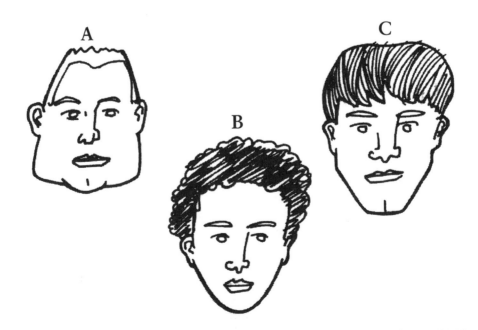

WHAT DO THESE FACES CONCEAL?

Test A

1. Does he listen to his feelings when making decisions?

2. Can this man work independently?

3. Does he take a great deal of care in his work?

4. Does he find it difficult to make friends?

5. Is money important for this man?

6. Would he be good at teaching?

7. Does this man always want to be the team captain?

Test B

1. Can this woman take criticism?

2. Is she ambitious at work?

3. Does she appear to be trusting?

4. Is she considered an optimist?

5. Does this woman need the admiration of others?

6. Would she be a good team player?

7. Does she dislike routine and seeks occupations that are stimulating and intriguing?

Test C

1. Does he have a quest for knowledge?

2. Is this person an optimist?

3. Does this person have enough stamina?

4. Is he material oriented?

5.   Does he lack self-confidence?

6.   Does he prefer permanent, quiet relationships?

A PERSONAL NOTE . . . ALICE

Our client, a victim of a tragic accident that left her a paraplegic at the age of 26, sat quietly in the courtroom. Her family was seeking medical expenses and round-the-clock care for her for the remainder of her life.

Naturally, as a jury consultant, my role was to determine which of the perspective jurors would be the least likely to identify with this case; which jurors would not be capable of awarding a fair sum of money to compensate for the girl's expenses so far and for her loss of future income as a registered nurse.

As I observed each prospective juror's face, my eyes rested on juror number 8 and I knew instantly that she would have to be deleted from the jury pool. She had an oval face, angular features, thin lips, thin hair and seemed to have a low estrogen level. Her handwriting, which was small and printed, further solidified my predispositioned negative feelings about her ability to sympathize with the victim. Her precise handwriting revealed that she would rely totally on facts, that she possessed very little compassion and that she would be negative to our case. In her occupation as a newspaper reporter, surely she was required to be factual and analytical, but in our case; she was HISTORY!

ANSWERS TO "WHAT DO THESE FACES CONCEAL?"

Test A

1.   No (face type)

2.   Yes (arched hair line)

3.   Yes (face shape)

4.   Yes (face shape)

5.   Yes (face type)

6.   No (hooked nose)

7.   Yes (square chin)

Test B

1.　　No (face type)

2.　　Yes (face type)

3.　　Yes (eyes wide set)

4.　　Yes (face shape)

5.　　Yes (large mouth)

6.　　Yes (flat eyebrows)

7.　　Yes (face shape)

TEST C

1.   Yes (wide forehead)

2.   No (facial expression)

3.   Yes (strong nose)

4.   Yes (face shape)

5.   No (face shape)

6.   Yes (protruding lower lip)

People Reading: The Body Language of Deceit

Years wrinkle the skin, but lack of enthusiasm wrinkles the heart.

Anyone whose livelihood depends upon knowing how other people are thinking, feeling and reacting should be keenly aware of nonverbal communication or body language. It is no accident that riverboat gamblers and high-stakes poker players wear sunglasses at the table—they know that their eyes can betray them. Whether it's a smile, eye movement or facial expression, the key to accurate personal perception is in the nonverbal response. Ninety-three percent of the time the true reaction of a person is carried in a nonverbal channel, and only seven percent of the time do people say what they really feel.

During voir dire, it is wise to give less weight to what people say and pay more attention to what they do not say. By the time a person reaches adulthood, he has become socially conditioned to follow conversational scripts and programs. He is often robot-like in his dialogues, giving standardized responses that are socially desirable and highly predictable. For example, when we are asked, "How are you?" We generally respond with the worn-out computerized, "Fine." Sometimes adults will present a social face that is widely dissimilar from their private feelings. Thus, the reading of an individual's nonverbal clues becomes an essential tool of attorneys and in the courtroom.

Nonverbal communication is any human reaction of feeling and attitude that is expressed in a body-language channel. These reactions are revealed in facial expressions, posture,

These reactions are revealed in facial expressions, posture, vocal intonation, eye movement, lines in the face or even in types of smiles. As our language message is being framed carefully for social approval, our emotions leak out into unobtrusive channels of the body. Bodily reactions occur even when we're quiet. As Freud said, "If his lips are silent, he chatters with his fingertips, betrayal oozes out of him at every pore."

THE BODY TALKS

When reading nonverbal cues to detect hidden messages, three guidelines will increase your accuracy of interpretation. First, a nonverbal movement, like folding arms, is significant only if it is a reaction to something. Many people cross their arms to rest them casually in a meaningless gesture. Second, the context within which a nonverbal response takes place should be used to give it meaning. For example, standing close to a friend would be a sign of intimacy and interest, but closeness to an individual during a sales meeting, or to a jury during final arguments, might be seen as high-pressure persuasion. Third, each nonverbal cue should be cross-checked with other nonverbal signs to ensure correct interpretation. For example, the disposition of the person who answers with a crisp "yes, sir," can be verified by rigid posture, tight lips and conservative dress. Increasing accuracy and developing competency at reading nonverbal cues requires an understanding of reaction, context and cross-checking of the signal.

LET'S GET PHYSICAL

Most basic communication gestures are the same all over the world. When people are happy, they smile; when they are sad or angry, they frown or scowl. Nodding the head is almost universally used to indicate "yes" or affirmation. Shaking the head from side to side to indicate "no" or negation is also universal and may well be a gesture that is learned in infancy. When a baby has had enough milk, he turns his head from side to side in rejection. But, just as verbal language differs from culture to culture, nonverbal language differs. Whereas one gesture may be common in a particular culture and have a clear interpretation, it may be meaningless in another culture or even have a completely opposite meaning.

One of the most serious mistakes a novice in body language can make is to interpret a solitary gesture in isolation from other gestures or other circumstances. Like any other language, body language consists of words, sentences and punctuation. Each gesture is like a single word and a word may have several different meanings. It is only when you put the word into a sentence with other words that you can fully understand its meaning. Gestures come in "sentences" and invariably tell the truth about a person's feelings or attitudes. A "perceptive" person is the one who can read the nonverbal sentences and accurately match them against the person's verbal sentences.

When we observe someone else, we first notice his physical appearance, and secondly, we notice his body language. Although the categories of appearance and body language may overlap, they often reveal very different aspects of a person's character. An individual can consciously choose his attire and determine, to a large degree, how his body will look, but most of his body language is beyond his control.

The manner in which someone combs his hair is a conscious choice, therefore it reveals how he wants to be seen. Someone's jewelry and accessories can supply clues about his religion, alma mater, degree of economic success, taste and much more. Clothing may point to a certain lifestyle choice; does the person prefer the practical or extravagant? Although physical appearance and body language usually provide different types of information, the knowledge that can be obtained from each of them is equally important. Sometimes appearance and body language point in the same direction, sometimes in opposite directions. The important point to remember is to simply pay attention to each and every detail when reading people.

Any trait that is extreme or that deviates from the norm is worth special attention. The same is true of any action or physical appearance that is inappropriate for a particular occasion. A halter top may be fine at the pool, but not at the company Christmas party or in the office. A conservative suit says one thing about a person when worn to church, quite another if worn to a child's baseball game. Further, a big smile and a slap on the back may be called for at a retirement party, but would raise questions at an interview.

Inappropriate clothing, makeup and hairstyles, as well as inappropriate gestures or other body motions, can reflect many things. Most commonly, the person may:

◆ be seeking attention.
◆ lack common sense.

◆   be attempting to imitate someone he admires.

◆   value comfort and convenience over all else (in the case of attire).

◆   not have been taught how to dress and act appropriately.

◆   be self-centered and insensitive to others.

◆   not have the proper attire for the occasion.

If someone's appearance or behavior seems inappropriate, take note of it and try to identify probable reasons.

MIRROR, MIRROR, ON THE WALL

Who's the fairest one of all? Physical appearance is important and is the first of many pieces used to fit together the puzzle of someone's character. Things, though, are not always what they seem. Just because someone wears a brightly colored outfit does not mean that he has a flamboyant personality and wants to be noticed. The outfit may be a gift or the wearer feels that it may camouflage his true feelings. A person who wears dark glasses inside may be doing so because he feels it is stylish rather than because he's hiding shifty eyes.

Even though every aspect of a person's appearance points in a different direction, adding and analyzing the individual's body language, environment, voice and behavior, one can safely conclude some findings. In cataloging a person's appearance for clues to his emotions, beliefs and values, careful analysis of the following most common features must be conducted.

◆   Physical characteristics (body, face, extremities, skin, and physical disabilities/irregularities)

◆   Ornamentation/jewelry

◆   Makeup

◆   Accessories

◆   Clothing

◆   "Bodifications" (elective alterations of the body)

◆   Hygiene

The only way to accurately interpret the meaning of these physical traits is to view them in context with other physical characteristics as well as mannerisms, environment, voice and actions.

Tan Skin

A tanned face may reveal that the person's job or hobbies put him outdoors for considerable periods. A tan may also indicate that someone is vain and appearance conscious, or that he has just returned from a vacation in a sunny location. To figure out which, you will have to observe other clues. For example, if the man is very tanned, deeply wrinkled and has calluses on his hands, he has probably spent a lot of time working outdoors. On the other hand, if he sports carefully manicured nails and an immaculate suit along with bronzed skin, the odds are that he thinks he looks better that way. It also can indicate that he has the time to pursue a dark tan.

Pale skin

A person whose skin is very pale generally has few outdoor hobbies and does not work outdoors. It is found that light-complected people with softer, paler skin tend to be less physically active and health conscious than those who show at least some exposure to the sun.

Irregularities

Facial irregularities such as moles or warts, particularly if they are conspicuous, are significant. Today most people have disfiguring blemishes removed. Sometimes these irregularities point to a socioeconomic background in which physical appearance is a very low priority. Often a person's reasons for retaining a facial blemish are more complicated. If someone does not bother to remove a large, dark mole from the tip of his nose, it may mean that he is extremely comfortable with himself, moles and all. Or it may show that he does not want to cater to an image-conscious society, in which case it may also reveal rebellious feelings.

Hygiene

Hygiene is one the most significant and noticeable traits. Poor hygiene reveals a wealth of information about a person, but it is essential to make the distinction between people who are unkempt and those who are dirty. Hygiene speaks of a person's education, social class, perception of himself and others, intelligence, organization, laziness, carelessness, security, self-image, rebelliousness, cultural background, consideration for others, desire to please and desire for social acceptance.

People with poor hygiene may be:

◆ oblivious to the effect they have on others. This indicates a high level of self-centeredness; a lack of common sense; or an inability to read the reactions of those around them.

◆ insensitive. They might know, but not care about the effect they are having on other people. This may indicate a lack of education or uncaring attitude toward others as well as self-centeredness.

◆ mentally ill or drug or alcohol abusers. Often, people who are depressed or have other chronic mental illnesses, including drug and alcohol abuse, ignore personal hygiene.

◆ unable to care for themselves because of a chronic medical problem.

◆ from a very poor socioeconomic background. Few people can not afford to be clean. But, some people raised in poverty were never taught the basics of personal hygiene, and occasionally they never pick up the habit of bathing regularly or putting on fresh clothes in the morning.

◆ lazy. Some people just do not want to make the effort to keep clean.

Fastidiousness

Fastidiousness in a person can be reflected in a perfectly trimmed beard, freshly pressed clothing, a precisely positioned pocket scarf or even in constant arranging and rearranging of clothing or desk items.

The more fastidious a person is, the more he will tend to be egotistical, structured, inflexible, unimaginative, vain and concerned about the opinions of others. Almost invariably, fastidious people have acquired the trait from their parents, therefore, fastidiousness usually reflects a strong parental influence.

Those on the opposite end of the spectrum who are flexible and easy going may wear shoes that are heavily scuffed and worn-out, shirts with holes, torn seams, missing buttons or pants with an unraveling hem.

Writing, Logos and Pictures on Apparel

Words or images displayed on clothing are virtual advertisements for someone's lifestyles and values. People do not randomly put on clothing with particular words, logos or pictures, rather, they choose what embodies their personality, depicts their interests or reflects an image they want to present.

◆ Prominently featured designer logos can indicate someone who is image conscious and perhaps lacks confidence. He may be trying to buy credibility with a designer label.

◆ Souvenir T-shirts from other cities, states and national parks may point out that the person is a traveler or outdoorsman.

◆ T-shirts or polo shirts with sports insignias can indicate someone who is either a fan or a player. His haircut and degree of athleticism will often tell which. Interestingly, some team logos have even been adopted by certain gangs as a type of uniform.

Careful analysis and attention to the details (writing, logo, picture) on clothing can reveal valuable hints as to the wearer's preferences and lifestyle.

Tattoos and Other "Bodifications"

Bodifications such as clothing and jewelry are temporary, just like the states of mind they may reflect. But, take notice when someone makes an affirmative decision to permanently alter his body with tattoos, implants or dramatic body piercing.

Tattoos are revealing on many levels. The subject matter alone is telling. A small flower may indicate that its wearer is trying to add beauty or interest to his life. Military personnel may get tattoos that symbolize their branch or unit. Regardless of their subject, large, obvious tattoos usually demonstrate:

◆ a need to be different

◆ rebelliousness

◆ nonconformity

◆ an artistic or bohemian nature

◆ membership in a peer group, such as the military or a gang

◆ lower socioeconomic or educational background

If someone has chosen to get a noticeable tattoo, it usually indicates that he is individualistic and a nonconformist. One can expect original thinking and spontaneity from this person. The bigger, brighter, bolder and more outrageous the tattoo or tattoos, the more they reveal these personality traits.

Noticeable body implants or facial surgery gives clues to an individual's personality. Each of the many ways someone changes or enhances his body, points toward what he values in himself and others. Someone who elects breast implants is typically vain and concerned about what others think of her. A man who has opted to have liposuction is rather conscious of his appearance and attractiveness. He probably is vain and typically financially secure enough to afford to be. As with tattoos, it is important to note the degree of any surgical enhancement. If the surgical alterations are what most people regard as outlandish, it is safe to conclude that the person's self-centeredness and emotionally needy nature would cloud his judgment and ability to accurately understand others.

Flamboyance versus Conservativeness

Flamboyance is characterized by bright colors, shocking or distinctive styles, eye-catching jewelry and the like. Conservatism is reflected by classic styles, subdued colors, and careful, meticulous grooming. Those who are flamboyant generally want to stick out; those who are conservative usually want to blend in. Flamboyance is one of those traits that can reflect polar opposites. Extremely flamboyant people can be confident and self-assured or they are insecure, lonely, needy and bored.

Whether they are lonely or confident, flamboyant people generally share a few characteristics. They:

◆   are creative, artistic and imaginative.

◆   usually have some money, since flamboyant clothing and jewelry are generally fairly expensive and not very practical.

◆   themselves are not severely practical.

◆   are nonconformists. They don't care what others think of them, as long as they have an audience.

◆   are independent.

Conservative people:

◆   are likely to care about the opinions of others, want to fit in and want to be accepted.

◆   are conformists who feel most comfortable when they meet social norms and expectations.

◆   are often practical, authoritarian and analytical.

◆   are conventional thinkers.

Practicality versus Extravagance

Anything that emphasizes comfort, cost or utility over style will point toward the practical person. Different features of a person's appearance help place him in one category or the other and each item must be taken into consideration in determining an individual's level of practicality versus his level of extravagance.

Does a woman wear matching accessories with her outfits, or prefer basic blacks and browns that are easy to coordinate? Does she have long, carefully painted, manicured nails or are they short and functional? Does she wear flats or high heels? Does she wear a lot of makeup which is expensive and time-consuming to apply?

Does a man wear color-coordinated ties, pocket scarves, socks or other clothing? Does he wear a carefree Timex watch or a heavy Rolex? Does he wear walking shoes or Italian loafers each day? Does he have his nails manicured? Does he get frequent haircuts, or does he allow his hair to grow a bit long before having it trimmed?

The nature of a person's toys also says something about whether he is practical or extravagant. Someone who golfs only rarely, but owns an expensive set of clubs is probably extravagant, not practical. The same can be said of someone who chooses an expensive, high-maintenance car.

People who are interested in comfort and practicality are usually:

◆   at ease with themselves and their position in life.

◆   not self-centered.

◆   willing to be nonconformists, if that is what it takes to be comfortable.

◆   frugal.

Extravagant people often:

◆   are image conscious.

◆   desire acceptance and approval.

◆   need the respect and admiration of others.

◆   genuinely enjoy "the gift of giving".

Before assuming whether someone has traits of extravagance or not, take a good look at where he spends his money. If he spends it where it will be very much in the public eye—on clothing, jewelry, cars, big parties and so forth—then he probably fits the extravagant profile. Less extravagant people spend money on things few people will see—for instance, on vacations, a summer house only his family will visit, or quiet contributions to his favorite charities.

BODY TYPES AND THE IMPRESSIONS THEY PROJECT

Since the body is a major tool used by a person to communicate and respond to other people, it requires one to form an awareness of what the shape, size and statue of a person communicates. Each body type—large, small, thin, hefty—possesses inherent image advantages and problems. Some body types maintain great power and force; they convey strength or weakness, superiority or inferiority, attractiveness or unattractiveness, and authority or lack of it. A body serves as an individual's means for measuring movement through time and space. Bodies exert force through weight and bulk. They experience pain and joy; they feel good; become ill; enjoy youth and grow old.

Stereotypes about physical attractiveness are determining factors in an individual's responses to others and their responses to him. Studies of attractiveness and persuasiveness show, for example, that audiences react more favorably to an appealing speaker. Attractive persons—those who understand and use their body type to maximum advantage, regardless of sex—achieve credibility easily.

Evidence shows, and experts in nonverbal communication agree, that people associate certain personality traits with specific body builds. These expectations exist and are part of the psychological mortar in interpersonal communication.

Interpersonal communications experts divide body types into three groups: endomorph, mesomorph and ectomorph. The endomorph is soft, round and fat—sometimes referred to as the hefty type. The mesomorph is muscular and athletic—referred to as the muscular or tall ideal. The ectomorph is also tall, but appears thin and fragile—referred to as the thin type. Between the basic three, combinations of the body types exist. Findings concerning personality traits of the various body types follow:

Endomorph (soft, round):

These individuals tend to be super heavy, with small hands and feet, a round face and body and a waist bigger than their shoulders.

They are food minded, home oriented, generous, happy and like to cook. They are procrastinators who are people oriented and need be accepted by others.

Meso-endomorph: Meso-endomorph individuals are stout, thick looking, somewhat heavy set and sport a strong chest.

They are freedom lovers who enjoy communication. They are doers, fun folks, who are optimistic, recognition motivated and generous. They tend to procrastinate and are not detailed oriented. These happy-go-lucky people are extremely compassionate jurors.

Mesomorph (muscular ideal): This body beautiful individual has square shoulders that are wider than his hips. He has strong arms and legs and is athletic.

These people are doers who are materially oriented. They are not overly generous, but are excellent business partners. They are good organizers with good follow-through. They like the outdoors; are competitive, dominant, self-centered, have low guilt levels and do not like to lose.

Meso-ectomorph: This type of person is linear and slender from head to foot. He does not skip meals and tends to watch his weight.

These individuals are technically oriented, picky, skeptical, conservative with what is theirs, but generous with what is others. They are escapist who are materially oriented and are not willing to risk themselves. They keep facts straight, have lots of drive and are loaded with talent. These perfectionists are price conscious and are willing to take calculated risks.

Ectomorph (tall, thin): These skinny individuals have long hands and feet. Their faces appear slim and narrow.

They are not physically oriented and are typically shy, reserved loners who do not like crowds. These thinkers are security motivated, perfectionists who are very gentle by nature. They make excellent teachers, professors or scientists.

There are indeed more variations than those listed that combine characteristics of the body type that they are most near. For research purposes, another category has been added:

Small or Short Person:
Some short people have a need to prove themselves, and often appear to have a chip on their shoulder. They may experience difficulty in looking mature and authoritative. They tend to be assertive and forceful to compensate for their lack of size.

WALKING TALL

Walking is a way of saying something when we are not saying a word.

Scurrying:
A quick walker is a mover who likes to accomplish as much as possible and go as many places as one can. He is usually an energetic, vital, vibrant person who is a doer. This dominant, straightforward type of walk indicates a positive, optimistic person.

Shuffling:
Walking slowly with dragging feet indicates one who is down to earth; with no phoniness or insincerity. He typically is a good, loyal, steadfast friend who can be counted on.

Slouch/drooped shouldered:
This walker, who is slightly bent over, shows a lack of confidence. He is modest, soft spoken and expects negative

| | happenings. He lacks positive self-esteem, feels "stepped on" and carries "muggability" around with him. |

Swinging: The slinky, sexy walker swings her hips to attract attention. She usually has many friends, is the life of the party and likes to be noticed.

Nose in the air: The person who walks with his nose in the air generally likes his space and prefers very few people around him. He likes to organize things rather than just being involved. Even though he seems superior, he is usually shy.

Military step: This person walks briskly, swings his arms and is a "no-nonsense" type. He is well organized, determined and in control. He knows what he wants in life, is goal oriented and is seldom distracted. He is involved with many projects and accomplishes a great deal.

DECODING VOCAL CLUES

By comparing a person's tone of voice with both his body language and words, one can determine his true emotions. When an individual's tone of voice, words and body language are in sync—when they fit a consistent pattern—it is fairly easy to interpret how he is feeling and predict how he will react to various situations. When the tone of voice and body language are at odds with each other or with the person's words, that's another matter.

Acoustic spetrography—voice identification—allows authenticity of tapes, gunshots, reconstruction of conversations and an analysis of events. It is used in cases ranging from murder and rape, to kidnapping, extortion and terrorism. Voice identification prints a picture of an individual's basic sound as his voice travels through his primary vocal tract. Every person has a unique "voice print." No two people can use the same vocal muscles in the same way and research indicates that it requires over 200 muscles to produce one single sound.

Understanding the messages encoded in vocal traits takes some practice and requires that the listener pay close attention. More than other traits, tone of voice shifts from second to second, depending on the environment and circumstances. While permanent traits such as a loud, booming voice may be fairly straightforward and easy to interpret, other, more transitory characteristics such as pitch, pace of speech and stammering can be harder to peg. In analyzing voices and their meaning, it is imperative to pay special attention to whether the tone matches or conflicts with the person's body language and words.

The most common voice traits are the most telling:

Loud voice: People with loud voices usually have acquired them for a reason. The key to evaluating the significance of a loud voice, is to assess when and how the person uses it and what he is attempting to accomplish by it.

Loudness is authoritative and intimidating and is often used to control the environment and those in it. In some cases, loudness is coupled with the practice of "speaking over" others, another attempt to control and one that suggests insensitivity and rudeness as well. Excessive dominance may also reflect egotism and impatience. Most people think those with loud, booming voices are displaying confidence. That may be the case, but some people shout because they are afraid no one will hear them if they whisper.

Generally speaking, people who have a loud, dominant voice, but use it courteously and appropriately are confident. Those who abuse others with their loud voice, like a bully with a big stick, are often insecure.

Soft voice: A soft voice can be used to manipulate others, or it can indicate a person who himself is easily swayed. While a low tone may initially suggest that the speaker lacks confidence and assertiveness, do not be fooled. A soft voice may reflect calm self-assurance: the speaker feels no need to dominate a conversation.

If the speaker has dropped his voice for a particular occasion, it could be that he is in an uncomfortable situation and feels nervous or intimidated. Some soft-speaking people use their voices as a power play by attempting to force someone else to come within earshot.

In evaluating a person with a consistently soft voice, one should focus on the appropriateness of whatever modulations exist. Does the person make an effort to speak louder when it is clear some of those present may not be able to hear him? If not, he may be unobservant, inconsiderate or arrogant. If the volume is low but he makes good eye contact and his body language is relaxed, the soft voice has little significance. If, on the other hand, the consistently low volume is combined with body language that reflects discomfort, such as lack of eye contact, turning the body or face away, or fidgeting, it would be correct to "read" the voice as a symptom of discomfort and lack of confidence.

Rapid speech: The phrase "fast-talking salesman" usually implies that someone is not only speaking rapidly, but frequently is not telling the truth. Excessively rapid speech does generally indicate untruthfulness when it is not the speaker's normal rate of speaking.

People who fast-talk all the time are usually tightly wound from the get-go. They are found to be as quick to assess and judge a situation as they are in expressing themselves. They tend to jump to conclusions quickly rather than carefully evaluate evidence. Fast talkers have a nervous personality and sometimes show signs of poor self-esteem.

Someone who normally speaks at an even pace, and begins to fast-talk, could be experiencing: nervousness, impatience, anxiety, insecurity, excitement, fear, anger, a desire to persuade or uneasiness over being caught in a lie.

Each of us has had the experience of being caught in a lie. We are usually chatting along at normal speed, then realize there is an inconsistency in our tale, and suddenly we switch to fast-forward as we try to explain ourselves. It is wise to be alert to the possibility that a fast-talker is trying to obscure the truth with a barrage of words—but it is much more likely that he is just nervous and insecure, and speaks quickly out of anxiety, or to make a point. This is evident in children when then become excited translating a story; usually, it is not much different with adults.

Slow speech: People who speak slowly tend to fall into one of two categories: those who sound and appear comfortable and relaxed; and those whose slow speech is accompanied by other physical and vocal clues suggesting discomfort. Normally people who speak slowly are those who analyze their thoughts before verbalizing them.

If someone usually speaks at a normal pace, and is speaking especially slow on a particular occasion, it may mean that he is trying to make a point that is important to him, confused, lying, fatigued, deep in thought, ill or sad and grieving. To decide which it is, the observer should consider the speaker's body language and the content of his speech.

Halting speech: Halting, hesitant or broken speech is different from slow speech. A stop-and-start pattern is usually caused by insecurity, nervousness or confusion. On occasion, it may reflect untruthfulness, as when someone struggles to come up with an excuse. But it can also point to the opposite direction: the speaker wants to be very accurate and is searching for just the right words.

To determine whether someone's halting speech signifies nervousness, confusion, untruthfulness, or an attempt at precision, examine the entire pattern of his speech, words and body language. People have to be pretty uptight about what they are saying for the tension to cause broken and halting speech. If they are lying, other signs will nearly always appear. Someone who is fibbing will lose eye contact, inadvertently cover his mouth or other parts of his face, or will fall prey to one of the other body language lying tip-offs discussed in this book. Assuming, though, that the speaker is not lying or nervous, for some, halting or broken speech is an honest struggle to simply articulate thoughts.

Pitch: People's voices range from calm and soothing to shrill and irritating. Vocal pitch is largely nonelective. Within the range that is normal for each of us, we raise and lower our pitch for a few standard reasons.

A person's voice will rise in pitch when he is especially scared, joyful, agitated or excited. If the feeling is intense enough, a person's voice will crack. In these cases, the cause is usually clear from accompanying body language, words and actions.

A person will noticeably lower his voice from its normal range when he is trying to seduce someone. Pitch may also drop when someone is sad, depressed or fatigued.

Flat, unemotional voice: A flat voice generally represents insincerity, boredom, anger, resentment, frustration, depression and some physical ailments. Sometimes the flat voice is the speaker's attempt to camouflage intense feelings of jealousy or resentment.

Hearing between the Lines: Spotting Mixed Messages

Anyone with normal hearing can detect the signals people convey with their tone of voice, but few of us understand all of them. This is partly because when we are interacting with someone, there is a lot of competition for our attention. We size up another person's appearance and body language, listen to the content of his message and watch his reactions to our words.

Hearing between the lines requires that an individual teach himself as to what to listen for. He can do so by:

◆ focusing on the voice—not the words—from time to time during the conversation.

◆ asking himself whether the voice reflects elective (voluntary) or nonelective (involuntary) characteristics.

◆ looking for patterns. Asking himself whether the voice is different now from its usual tone or is it in any way exaggerated.

◆ comparing the voice to the person's body language and words.

◆ considering the environment.

◆ decoding the vocal clues.

A Personal Note . . . Alice

I was asked to assist in the selection of participants for a program being initiated in a minimum-security prison. It was a rehabilitation program sponsored by several chefs.

My responsibility was to determine, through their handwriting, which of the prisoners, not only qualified for the program, but who would be the best "team" players and who would be the best leaders.

After my analysis, the warden notified me that my findings mirror imaged those of the two psychologists who had also been asked to give data and conclusions about the inmates. I was eventually sent a picture of the group, actually dressed in their chef uniforms, and was able to identify almost every inmate by the previous study that I had made of their handwriting samples.

People who possess high manual dexterity will create writing that contains well-rounded *m*'s, and *n*'s and squared-off *r*'s.

Actions Speak Louder Than Words

You can preach a better sermon with your life than with your lips.

She's short, dark-haired, average weight, well-dressed, smiles a lot, has three college degrees. She is single with no children, is a speaker, belongs to several professional associations, loves shopping and reading, speaks with a Southern accent, comes from a close family and is the middle child of three. She has a thousand other characteristics and I have five minutes to decide whether she can give my client a fair trial. So many clues, so little time!

Courtroom consultants often face this type of pressure and a wrong decision can literally be fatal to their clients. With so much to look at, the only way to reach a meaningful conclusion about someone's personality or beliefs is to focus on those traits and characteristics that will most likely predict how a person thinks and behaves.

READING READINESS

No trait or characteristic means the same thing in every person or in every circumstance, but some characteristics do consistently tell more than others. The three key traits that provide consistently reliable insight into almost everyone, almost all the time are:

1. compassion

2. socioeconomic background

3. satisfaction with life

Compassion

These traits are blind to race, gender, age, sexual orientation and other characteristics by which we often stereotype those who belong to an identifiable group. Concentrating on these traits forces one to look through any stereotype and to the person's underlying qualities and experiences.

When evaluating someone, one of the first things to do is to place him on an imaginary compassion measurement scale. On one end is the cold, unemotional, uncaring person; on the other is the warm and compassionate soul. Where a person finds himself on the scale can divulge more about how he is likely to think and behave, than any other single fact.

The closer people are to the compassionate end of the scale, the more they tend to be generous, fair, sincere, affectionate, family-oriented, forgiving and understanding of human frailty. They are inclined to give others the benefit of the doubt and are more inquisitive and patient than people who lack compassion. They dislike hurting anyone, therefore, they are unlikely to be dishonest. They tend to believe that what goes around, comes around.

People who fall on the uncaring end of the scale tend to be more critical, intolerant, unforgiving, harsh, punitive and self-centered. They are also frequently more analytical and more likely to scan the facts then make a quick decision. By the same token though, they tend to be more judgmental, impulsive and inclined to act before all the information is in.

Socioeconomic Background

A person born with a silver spoon in his mouth will almost always view life differently from someone born and raised in poverty, regardless of what other characteristics they may share. But socioeconomic background is not measured only by family income. It consists of a combination of social and economic factors. The love and support one receives as a child, his exposure to learning and other worldly experiences, the environment in which he was raised and a thousand other factors come into play. An individual's attitude toward life is greatly influenced by whether or not his emotional and physical needs have been fulfilled.

People who have had difficulty in achieving success, whether financial or emotional, may develop an attack mentality and retain it all their life, no matter how much money or success they eventually achieve. They occasionally become hardened and lack confidence. They may be insecure, unkind, inconsiderate, stingy, intolerant, defensive and unwilling to reveal much of themselves. Because they have had to fight so hard to survive, they tend to be more watchful and to believe the ends justify the means. On the positive side, those who have pulled themselves up by the bootstraps also tend to be focused, hardworking and dedicated to achieving their objectives.

People who have always had their needs fulfilled, on the other hand, tend to be more confident, secure, kind, generous, tolerant, forgiving and open. But, if life has been easy and everything has been handed to them, they occasionally lack drive and intensity and have a tendency to be rather materialistic and egocentric.

A person who experiences prejudice as a child, is likely to become suspicious and defensive. If a person lives with constant criticism, he is more likely to become judgmental and intolerant. If someone is treated with kindness and compassion, he will probably become caring. If he had to struggle to make ends meet, he may become less giving. It doesn't matter whether someone's tall or short, black or white, male or female, young or old, his socioeconomic background is a key predictive trait to his behavior.

Satisfaction with Life

An individual's satisfaction with life has a wide-ranging effect on how he thinks and how he treats others. People who have achieved their goals tend to believe in personal accountability and responsibility. They are optimistic, compassionate, supportive and at peace with themselves and others. They also tend to be more forgiving, hardworking and industrious.

Those who have not achieved their goals often possess a victim mentality. They are quick to place blame on others and may be bitter, angry, negative, pessimistic and vengeful. Usually, they are less industrious and more critical and cynical than achievers.

It is usually not difficult to find out how satisfied someone is. A few simple questions such as, "What did you want to be when you were in high school?" or "How do you like your job?" or "If you could change your life, what would you do?" will usually prompt responses that make it clear whether someone has achieved personal success.

READING THE HIDDEN MESSAGES OF THE BODY

Like physical characteristics, most body movements can have many meanings or no meaning at all, depending on the circumstances. The best way, though, to sort the meaningful information from the unimportant details is to learn how various emotions are typically revealed, and then search for abnormalities in behavior when studying a particular person.

Charlie Chaplin and many other silent movie actors were the pioneers of nonverbal communication skills. Body language was the only means of communication on the screen and each actor was classed as good or bad by the extent to which he could use gestures and other signals to communicate effectively. When talking films became popular and less emphasis was placed on the nonverbal aspects of acting, many silent movie actors faded into obscurity and those with good verbal skills prevailed.

Researchers agree that the verbal channel is used primarily for conveying information, while the nonverbal channel is used for negotiating interpersonal attitudes, and in some cases is used as a substitute for verbal messages. Much of our basic nonverbal behavior is learned and the meaning of many movements and gestures is culturally determined. In fact, up to the age of three, children rely heavily on nonverbal messages to communicate with one another.

One reason for the importance of visual information in any exchange, and the reason why success of all kinds depends more on silent speech than verbal eloquence, comes from the relative importance of the visual and auditory systems. Faced with the hypothetical alternative of going either deaf or blind, more than 95 percent of people opt for deafness.

In the unfamiliar, austere and intimidating atmosphere of the courtroom, prospective jurors tend to be very restrained in their verbal responses, while physical responses and movements go unrestrained. It is this Kinesic behavior, or nonverbal communication, that often indicates to the trained observer important characteristics concerning a prospective juror's attitudes, personality and biases. Careful observation of a juror's body movements and facial expressions in response to questions (or, his behavior while not being questioned) can lead to a better interpretation of what the juror is or is not truthfully verbalizing. Observing and interpreting body movements such as eye contact, hand movement, posture, gestures and vocal intonation can provide trial counsel with key additional information about each juror.

THE EYES: WINDOWS TO THE SOUL

The eyes have a language all their own. Expressions such as, "He gave her the evil eye." "She had a gleam in her eye." or "His eyes danced with joy." illustrate the variety of feelings expressed by the eyes. It has long been believed that a person's eyes hold the key to his innermost thoughts and feelings.

The pupillary reflex, which is the sudden widening or narrowing of the pupils, reveals that an individual's pupils will dilate when he sees something he likes, constrict when he looks at something distasteful or uninteresting, and remain unchanged when he is indifferent. In dimly lighted, smoke-filled rooms where card sharks ply their trade, decisions of whether to hold or fold often have been made by studying the eyes of the other players in the game.

The Arabs have know about pupil response for hundreds, if not thousands, of years. Since people can not control the response of their eyes, which is a dead giveaway, many Arabs, like Arafat, wear dark glasses, even indoors. It is believed that magicians can pick out the card an audience member is thinking about by watching the person's pupils widen as the card comes up. Maybe used car salesmen, who are accustomed to customers playing it cool and acting disinterested, should simply wait until the customer's pupils dilate once he reaches the car he really wants, then pitch his sales dialogue. Exotic women attempting to entice men, have, for ages, used their understanding of pupil dilation in reverse. Knowing that a dilated pupil communicated interest, excitement, softness and warmth, they often dilated their own eyes with a drug to increase the size of their pupils.

In applying the pupillary phenomenon to the courtroom, keep in mind the following five points:

1.   When a person's pupils enlarge, he is responding emotionally.

2.   In most instances, enlarged pupils indicate interest, liking, attention, excitement or arousal.

3.   If a person is shocked or horrified, his pupils will widen briefly, then slowly narrow.

4.   If a person becomes extremely angry, which will be obvious by his demeanor, his pupils will suddenly become large as a part of a fight/flight response.

5.   Wide-eyed people are chronically excited and easily become emotional, whereas beady-eyed people tend to be colder, unemotional, more rational and businesslike.

As veniremen are summoned in the courtroom, it is interesting to note their eyes. Wide-eyed people, who are typically emotional and easily moved to pity, empathy and compassion, are usually good for plaintiffs in personal injury cases, and may be favorable jurors for a criminal defense that involves a nonviolent, pathetic-looking defendant. Often, these individuals rely on intuition and subjective feelings in making decisions.

Beady-eyed persons, on the other hand, with extremely small pupils, tend to be cool and businesslike. They are guided by hard, cold logic and reason. Paper boys hoping for a tip should not waste much time in the doorway talking to this type of person. Attorneys, looking for a sizable award, should also look elsewhere.

If possible, during questioning, the attorney should stand directly in front of each juror as he asks a question. This way the attorney can determine whether the juror's eyes dilate or constrict as he approaches. If the juror's eyes widen and remain that way, he probably likes the attorney or finds him interesting or exciting. A juror whose pupils constrict, may feel rejection and a dislike for the attorney. If a juror's pupils remain the same, it is a signal that he is neutral or indifferent. This same information can be used in the courtroom when pointing out the defendant to the jury or during cross-examination of a witness. An attorney who wants to know if he is getting to a witness, should move close to him and watch his pupils. If the witness feels danger, his pupils will dilate as the pressure become more intense. If the witness's pupils remain small or medium in size, then he is composed.

Eye Movement: Right Lookers and Left Lookers

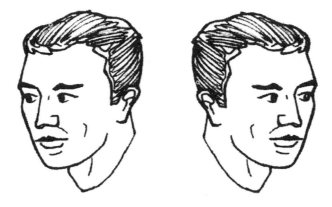

The joint movement of the eyes to the upper right or upper left during mental reflection is called conjugate lateral eye movement. People are classified as right-lookers (movers) or left-lookers on the basis of the predominant direction of their eye movements when they are required to think or solve a problem. Judges, jurors and attorneys who typically look right are very different from those who look left.

The favored direction a person looks or moves when pondering something reveals the predominant hemisphere he uses to solve problems. The left brain controls eye movement to the right and the right brain produces eye movement to the left. It is understood that the left hemisphere is associated with speech, logic, reason, factual information, mental arousal, analytical thinking and objectivity; while the right brain is primarily emotional, visual, artistic, musical, poetic, metaphoric, intuitive, passive, spatial and subjective. Consequently, a person who always looks to the right (left brain) when deliberating may be preoccupied with logic in making his decisions, and a left-looking person (right brain) typically turns inward to draw upon subjective matters, memory and emotions to help him to reach a decision that feels is right.

When talking to a right-looking (left brain) judge in the courtroom, it is wise to use hard, cold logic in an efficient, orderly style. When appealing to a left-looking (right brain) judge, visualizations, analogies and emotional pleas are advisable. With the logical judge, facts should be presented in an A . . . . B . . . . C . . . . style and with the intuitive judge, it is wise to present visualizations and use sentences such as, "Your Honor, can you *see* . . . ?" Classifying a judge as a right-looker or as a left-looker makes it possible to design language to better fit his psychological makeup and cognitive style.

During jury selection, it is also important to differentiate left-lookers from right-lookers. Those who look mostly left during questioning tend to be more favorable for the plaintiff, because they rely more on feelings and intuition in making decisions. Right-lookers, on the other hand, are better for the defense, since they are more cerebral and logical.

Eye Contact and Gaze Aversion

Customs officials are taught to watch the eyes of the person they are questioning when inquiring about goods being brought into the country. If the traveler maintains eye contact while describing his foreign purchases, it is taken as a sign of truthfulness. However, should the returning tourist look down and away, as he awkwardly says, "Yes, one bottle of rum is all I am declaring," the customs officer may buzz for officials in the back room. Gaze aversion, which is looking down and to the side (usually to the right) is interpreted to mean doubt, discomfort, anxiety, uneasiness or guilt, in situations of confrontation.

In the courtroom, a witness who is ill at ease with parts of the cross-examination will usually break eye contact and look down, as will a prospective jury member who is uneasy. If a witness repeatedly avoids the attorney's gaze, it is wise to conclude that he is being deceitful. Like the traveler with illegal goods going through customs, the gaze averter has something to hide, an attitude that he does not want anyone to know about.

Jury members who refuse to look the attorney in the eye anticipate dominance, intimidation or disapproval. If one attorney can arouse no contact, but the opposition succeeds in drawing the same person's glances, it is safe to conclude that one of that attorney's strikes has now been determined.

Moderate eye contact is what should be expected. When someone temporarily breaks eye contact, it means that he is either processing what was said or forming a response to a question. In either case, he is interested and involved in the conversation taking place. The brief interruption in eye contact shows that the listener is mentally paying attention to the proceedings and the repeated return of his eyes to the speaker, demonstrates ongoing interest.

High levels of eye contact indicate unusual attraction to someone. Hollywood directors who wish to convey feelings of love will often show a couple locked in a long, spellbound look. Whether it is a romantically involved couple, two close friends, or strangers with a natural attraction, a high level of easy eye contact is an indication of warm feelings and a desire to affiliate.

Beware, though, of the person with the long glance. When a person violates social custom with extended gazing devoid of friendly gestures, it is interpreted as defiance, dislike, anger or hostility. In some instances, the starer may want to blatantly threaten another with his burning look. In either case, strike out jurors with exceeding long, glaring stares.

The Sharpshooter's Eye

When a hunter gets ready to pull the trigger of his rifle, he squints the corner of his eye to increase his level of concentration and directs his focus on the target. The more intense his attention the more he squints. When eyes are tightened and slant downward at the outer corners, the sharp shooter effect is created. This nonverbal response reveals an attitude of skepticism and criticalness that demands a high degree of exactitude. These people are inclined to be attentive to details and constantly measure the accuracy of others, always ready to take aim on anyone lacking pinpoint accuracy. When the attorney knows that the burden of proof is on himself and his evidence is a little light, he should keep the sharpshooter off the jury.

The individual with the sharpshooter's eye, though, should be retained on a jury:

1. When an attorney has a good case with a systematic, orderly presentation.

2. If the trial attorney himself, is by nature, precise and methodical.

3. When a defense attorney wants to lower an inevitable compensatory award by having a stickler for details play the devil's advocate on the jury to force a lower compromise verdict.

Eyeblink

Imagine yourself in an elegant restaurant with friends and the flawlessly dressed waiter drops his fountain pen on your nice white shirt. Probably you would have noticed that your eyes blink at this unexpected incident. Just as the eyeblink protects us from the physical harm of unpredictable missiles endangering our vision, it can also act to blunt the impact of a psychological threat by cutting off the reality. The more persistent the threat, the more frequent will be the eyeblinks. Excessive eyeblinks are correlated with anxiety provoking interactions or situations.

Counting the number of eyeblinks can be a good measure of how much anxiety an individual is generating in a courtroom. The average rate of blinking for humans in lubricating the eyeball, is about 12 times per minute. A substantial departure from this rate is indicative of a state of tension or uneasiness, in which the eyeblink helps the person to break contact with the offensive source.

During jury selection, it is wise to notice if anyone blinks excessively during questioning. Which of the attorneys cause the jurors to blink more? When the crime that was committed is mentioned or as the personal injury is being described, which jurors blink more? The eyeblink can also be used to monitor the reactions of the jurors to particular key witnesses in a trial. The more times a person blinks his eyes, the less favorable he feels about a person or an incident.

As economics dictate, corporations that are the defendants, have been employing forensic psychologists and human behavior analysts to monitor juror reactions as each segment of evidence is presented; eyeblinks included. At every recess, corporate attorneys may check with the expert monitors to find out how jurors are responding. With this information, fine adjustments can be made as the trial progresses and final summations can be tailored more to fit the minds of the jurors.

THE NOSE KNOWS

In body language, the nose is not as versatile or mobile as the eyes, the hands, or the mouth, yet it speaks volumes. Whether we wrinkle it, touch it, rub it, or pinch it; we impart a definite, although secret, message to the person with whom we are conversing.

Nose Wrinkle

The most obvious expression with the nose is to wrinkle it in disgust. In the case of extreme disgust, the cheeks rise, causing the eyelids to narrow. This nasal expression resembles that which occurs when a person gets a whiff of an unpleasant smell. When this motion is done, perhaps the disgusted person is saying "this really smells!" When jurors hear evidence that they strongly reject, the nose wrinkle is evident.

The Nose Touch

A less obtrusive nose gesture that usually goes unnoticed in ordinary conversation, is the nose touch or rub. It is accomplished by placing the index (usually left) finger on the left side of the nose, crooking it under the nose, or using it to rub the nose. Whether it is a touch or rub on the side or bottom of the nose, it means the same thing, namely, "What I'm telling you stinks!"

Nose touching is a sign of falsehood and evasion. Scientific observers and body language scholars, along with Desmond Morris, author of *Manwatching*, state: "Nose touching and deceit go together in a remarkable way . . ."

Why does a deceiver go to his nose when he fibs, lies or expresses counterfeit feelings? Morris proposes two explanations: (a) A person whose inner feelings and thoughts are in conflict with outer demeanor and speech will experience slight tension. This discomfort causes a minor physiological change in the lining of the nasal cavity, making it more sensitive and itchy. And, (b) When an untruth is spoken, the person's hand unconsciously will go to his mouth as if to keep the fraudulent words from coming out. He does not want to be the one to "spill the beans." Since the mouth cover is so transparent, he, in a split second will move the hand that was headed for the mouth, past the mouth, and brings it to rest casually on his nose. Consequently, what starts as a mouth-cover movement to stop his lying, ends up as an innocent nose touch, keeping his true feelings and the meaning of his words hidden.

The final shift from mouth to nose may be due to an unconscious sensation that mouth-covering is too obvious—a motion that most children do when they're telling untruths. Touching the nose, as if it is itching, may therefore be a disguised mouth-cover—a cover-up of the cover-up.

Since jurors are not allowed to speak, those who tap, rub or touch their nose may be letting the attorney know how they feel in the only way they can. What all cases of involuntary nose-touching do have in common is that, the performer is reacting emotionally to the fleeting stress of deceit.

Pinching the Bridge of the Nose

A person experiencing inner conflict and turmoil will often close or squint his eyes, lower his head, and pinch the bridge of his nose. A judge cannot announce to both attorneys "Give me a little time to agonize over this decision; I'm uncertain as to what to do." However, when the judge feels that he is caught between two compelling arguments, he may externalize this feeling by pinching the bridge of his nose between his thumb and forefinger. Closing the eyes serves to break contact from the conflict and lowering the head shows the heaviness of the decision weighing on the judge's mind. Pinching the bridge gives the message "I can't see it and it's giving me a headache!"

WHAT'S BEHIND A SMILE

The most confusing facial gesture is the smile. If Leonardo's Mona Lisa were smiling from the jury box, would you know if she liked you or not? Is she sneering, smirking, conveying contempt or warmth? Would she be aloof or loving, warm or cold? Most smiles are not quite as hard to figure out, but many are difficult. Smiles do not always signify that the person feels happiness, warmth and liking.

While at least 19 different smiles exist, most of the value for trial attorneys will come from learning the five basic types of smiles that are produced by feelings of hollowness, pleasurable delight, pessimism, uncertainty and hostility.

The Hollow Oblong Smile

The oblong or hostess smile is formed by wrapping the parted lips horizontally around the teeth. In other words, the corners of the mouth are not pulled upward, but are simply stretched back toward the rear molars. Flight attendants, hostesses, politicians, Hollywood actors and con artists who must charm others, flash this attractive, but dishonest, smile. It looks great, but it means nothing. In a genuine smile or laugh, the eyes close somewhat or squint; with this one, the eyes remain more open. The horizontal smile gives the message, "I'm smiling at you just to be polite." This is also the smile that is displayed when one is pretending to enjoy a joke.

The Smile of Pleasurable Delight

Positive feelings can be reflected in three types of smiles: simple smiles, upper smiles and broad smiles. Each of these smiles is spontaneous and represents different degrees of pleasurable delight. The simple smile is when the lips curl up and back, but are not parted, so there are no teeth showing. It occurs when someone is enjoying a private joke.

The upper smile is a gracious smile of easy friendliness with the top teeth exposed. This smile usually takes place when one person is being introduced to another person. It is as though the smiling person is saying, "Hello, it's good to meet you."

The broad smile, with lips wide apart, mouth fully open and all the teeth showing, signifies the greatest degree of pleasure. This expression conveys favorable surprise or joyful delight over something. In true smiles, a person's lips are turned upward and his eyes sparkle.

The Turned-Down Smile of Pessimism

The smile of pessimism is indicated by a mouth that is faintly turned down at the corners, similar to that of a half moon. People with this type of smile anticipate a dark, gloomy future, have a pessimistic attitude and tend to be conservative. Therefore, jurors wearing the smile of pessimism are thought to be extremely frugal in their personal injury verdicts.

Biting the Lip in Uncertainty

Although it is hard to consider it a smile, biting the lower lip or the lip-in gesture is included as one of the basic smiles because the upper teeth are bared. It is formed by making the upper smile and then tucking the lower lip in, between the teeth. This type of smile means that the person doing the biting is in an uncertain state. When a person cannot decide on something, he bites his lower lip, expressing doubt. In certain contexts, this type of smile is seen on the face of a coy woman as she plays a child's role in trying to manipulate someone else. An uncomfortable feeling that a juror has about the presentation of some of the evidence in a trial, may manifest itself in the lip-in smile. Either way, it is a sign that suggests the individual is in a state of doubt.

The Forced Smile of Hostility

When feelings of hostility or dislike mix with efforts to be socially polite, strange smiles result. Forced smiles cause the eyes to squint; almost as though the person has been squirted in the eyes with a grapefruit. The grapefruit smile is taut with tension and the eyes narrow tightly in a painful squint at the corners. A person who dislikes others, but must pretend friendliness will show a grapefruit smile. Expect no sympathy or understanding from the person who constantly smiles in this way.

EMOTIONS OF THE FACE

Identify each of the following emotions illustrated.

(a) Happiness   (d) Anger

(b) Sadness   (e) Fear

(c) Disgust/contempt   (f) Interest

The answers to "Emotions of the Face" are found at the end of this chapter.

THE LANGUAGE OF HEAD POSITIONS

The manner in which a person holds his head can tell you whether he is of high-status and if he is interested in what is being said.

Backward Tilt

Maitre d's of exclusive eating places can identify people of importance or pedigree background by the backward tilt of their head. Snobbish people, those who feel superior or elite will tilt their heads back, half close their eyes and literally look down their nose at others. Thus, high-status people carry their heads high and are easy to pick out walking into a restaurant or into the jury box. They keep their nose up in the air and their bodies are erect. With their assumed posture, which often goes unnoticed, they are unconsciously conveying their arrogance and aristocratic authority. They command immediate respect and want to influence others with their ideas.

Side Tilt

When an animal suddenly hears a strange noise that he is curious about, he perks up his ears and cocks his head. Darwin observed that both animals and humans tilt their heads sideways whenever they hear something interesting. It may be that this position change is an instinctive attempt, like a radar scanner, to locate the exact source of the sound with the ear, thereby increasing auditory clarity. When the head tilt occurs, it is a clue that something has caught the attention of the listener.

THE LANGUAGE OF HAND GESTURES

Hands and arms provide even more accurate clues to hidden feelings than the face does. To some extent, a person can control his facial expressions, but his true feelings do leak out through his hands, arms and body. R. Harrison, author of *Beyond Words: An Introduction to Nonverbal Communication*, so aptly put it when he said, "The hands and feet do not 'talk' as much as the face, but they tell the truth."

Steepling

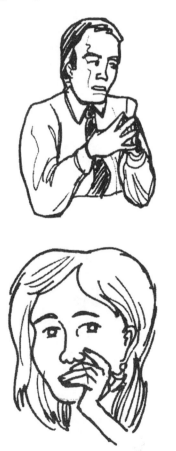

This gesture is made by unobtrusively placing the thumb and forefingers together in the shape of a steeple or castle. Steepling is a sign of a person with a smug, superior, regal, authoritative or political attitude. Watching someone peering out over his symbolic castle, gives the impression that he is sitting on a throne. The greater the authority, the more likely a person is to steeple while he delivers his "pearls of wisdom."

People who are overly confident in their authority or position are likely to steeple with countless frequency. Religious leaders, physicians, judges, lawyers and others whose advice has impact, often steeple while giving their opinion.

The more confident a person is, and the more important he thinks he is, the higher he steeples. Women tend to steeple low, sometimes with their steeple held down in their lap. Some people steeple as high as chest level, and still others at chin level.

The significance of the steepling gesture during jury selection is its usefulness in helping to ascertain the probable leaders on the jury; those who have authoritarian inclinations. These confident people are usually good for the prosecution and bad for the criminal defense, especially if they are looking at you over half glasses.

Frequency of steepling will indicate how strongly a person will defend his position. A snooty head tilter with thin lips and beady eyes, who steeples a lot, is expected to dish up a small award and dare anyone to challenge his decision. A wide-eyed, full-lipped man, with a warm smile and fleshy body, who steeples, is quite different. He typically would vigorously defend a big award for the plaintiff who is hurt.

Closed Hands

The obvious sign of anger is a clenched fist. Its meaning is so clear that it is used worldwide as a sign of hostility, force, power and intimidation. Politicians and national leaders make it part of their speeches to show the populace that they are determined to make good their pledges. It is doubtful that any juror will blatantly push a raised fist in an attorney's face when he does not agree with what was said. Instead, his hands will be closed unobtrusively and hidden behind his back, under his armpits, in his lap or in his pockets.

When hands close, no matter how slightly; it indicates anger and conflict. After all, people make fists when preparing for combat, don't they?

Open Hands

While closed hands represent a closed, rigid mind; open hands are the opposite: a sign of openness. Someone unconsciously throwing his hands open to his sides with his palms up, seems to be saying; like the child whose mother asks, "What are you hiding?" "See, I'm not hiding anything." Although actors consciously do it for effect, most people are unaware that when they are being candid and frank in their replies, they turn their palms up. By this gesture, they are showing that they are not palming any aces or hiding information. Similar to gate doors being swung open, allowing passage, hands and arms moving to the side makes someone more accessible to questions. The odds are good that a juror who opens his hands while answering is being honest and open in handling questions.

The Finger Point

When someone points his finger at you while answering one of your questions, you normally feel some slight discomfort. Everyone points on various occasions to punctuate an idea or to direct attention to an object. However, those to whom it is second nature may be hiding authoritarian tendencies. Repeatedly, it has an intimidating effect and represents aggressive inclinations. Some people cock it like a gun, with the thumb up, before they point it. It is no coincidence that the pointed finger symbolizes a weapon to the receiver of the point.

Teachers keep students in line with their pointed index fingers; clergymen counsel their flock with it; drill sergeants get their point across by sticking their finger in the chests of their recruits; and parents use it to stress each important segment of their "lecture." Authoritarians in the jury box unconsciously do it to lawyers who dare question them. At the very least, it signifies intensity in making a point, and at its worst, it is a vehicle of hostility, power and authority. A finger pointer will usually be favorable for the prosecution and deadly for the defense, because he is so intensely dedicated to control and conformity.

HANDSHAKE STYLES

Shaking hands is a relic of the caveman era. Whenever cavemen met, they would hold their arms in the air with their palms exposed to show that no weapons were being held or concealed. This palms-in-air gesture became modified over the centuries and numerous other variations developed. The modern form of this ancient greeting ritual is the interlocking and shaking of the palms. In most English-speaking countries, it is performed both on initial greeting and on departure and the hands are normally pumped three to seven times.

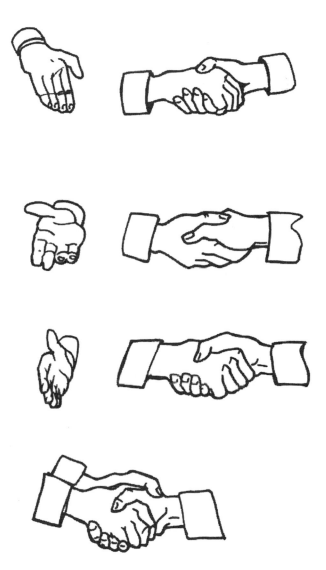

One of three basic attitudes is transmitted unconsciously through the handshake. Dominance is transmitted by turning the hand so that the palm faces down in the handshake. The palm need not be facing the floor directly, but if it is facing downwards in relation to the other person's palm, it is indicative of a wish to take control in the encounter that follows.

Just as the dog shows submission by rolling on its back and exposing its throat to the aggressor, so does the human as he uses the palm-up gesture to show submission to others. Therefore, the reverse of the dominant handshake is to offer your hand with your palm facing upwards. This handshake is particularly effective when you want to allow the other person to feel that he is in control of the situation.

When two dominant people shake hands, a symbolic struggle takes place as each person tries to turn the other's palm into the submissive position. The result is a vice-like handshake with both palms remaining in the vertical position as each person transmits a feeling of respect and rapport to the other. This vice-vertical palm grip is the handshake a father teaches his son when showing him how to "shake like a man."

The glove handshake, placing your two hands around the right hand of another, is sometimes called the politician's handshake. In this instance, the initiator tries to give the receiver the impression that he is trustworthy and honest, but typically when this handshake is used on a person he has just met, it has the reverse effect. The receiver feels suspicious and cautious about the initiators intentions. The glove handshake should only be used with people to whom the initiator is well-known.

The knuckle grinder, a handshake in which an excessively tight hold is used to grasp the receiver's hand, is the trademark of the aggressive "tough guy" type. Unfortunately, there are no effective ways to counter it, apart from a verbal mention of the pain it causes or a twitch of discomfort in the receiver's face. Like the palm-down thrust, the stiff-arm thrust tends to be used by aggressive types. Its main purpose is to keep another at a distance and out of the initiator's intimate zone.

Few greetings, though, are as uninviting as the dead fish handshake, particularly when the hand is cold or clammy. The soft, placid feel of the dead fish makes it universally unpopular. Most people relate it to weak character, mainly because of the ease with which the palm can be turned up. Surprisingly, many people who use the dead fish handshake are unaware that they do so.

SPEAK MY MIND: HAND GESTURES THAT REVEAL YOUR THOUGHTS

Hands to the Face

To ensure that an individual's hands will not give him away, when he feels the urge to silence a boring individual who's talking him to death, he uses them in a variety of ways. He might tie his hands up in the activities of smoking, drinking or clicking a pen. He may even hide them in his pockets or he may even try to freeze his potentially revealing hands by locking his fingers together. Most people bring their hands to their face so they can be marginally aware of them. Once hands are placed on the face, though, they are almost forgotten. What a person does not realize is that his inner thoughts, feelings and attitudes are disclosed by the position of his hands on his face.

The hands-to-the-face gestures is an unusually rich source of information. The face contains four different sense organs, and the specific organ that the hand goes to, indicates whether the person unconsciously wants to intensify what he is seeing, hearing, smelling or saying.

Hands-to-the-face movements are of special value in the courtroom where only the top portions of the bodies of witnesses, jurors and the judge usually are visible.

Hands in Pockets

When an individual places his hands in his pockets and keeps them there for an extended period of time, he may feel dejected or depressed. Once his hands are in his pockets and he begins to jingle the change that he finds there, it is highly indicative of the burden he is feeling concerning his financial condition. Money is important to him in his life; he either has a great deal of it and is thinking about making even more. Or, he is deeply in debt and very anxious about earning more money. This financial burden is further illustrated during Christmas season when people on the street jingle change in buckets to announce their need for more coins.

Finger-in-the-Cheek

A juror or judge who places his index finger on his cheek pointing upward, and keeps his remaining fingers wrapped about his chin, is giving careful consideration to and scrutinizing the proceedings. He is a critical thinker who is thoughtfully weighing the evidence. The index finger is pointing toward the eye as if to say, "Let me see . . . " The gesture itself neither connotes a negative nor a positive appraisal, it simply means an evaluation is taking place. Additional clues, such as forward lean/backward lean, arms cross/arms open, can suggest whether the evaluator is pondering the evidence in a positive or a negative way.

When the thinking person has concluded his evaluation, watch for him to assume a new pose. It is this posture that immediately follows the thinker position that may be the significant one. He may break out of the hand-cheek touch and move into a folded-arms posture, signifying resistance. Or, if he is favorable to the information he has just heard, he might tilt his head while thinking and then position his arms in an open, casual posture shortly thereafter. By studying the finger-cheek sequel, an attorney can often determine how the evidence is being graded.

The Chin Stroke

A man will stroke his chin or beard when he is deep in thought. Although the chin stroke is similar to the cheek touch, the chin stroke is thought to be a softer meditative state. Stroking, by its very nature, is a soothing action which implies easy thinking that is relatively free of conflict. Chin stroking, then, is associated with a nonjudgmental, reflective state, while the cheek touch discloses that a critical mind is making fine discriminations. Chin strokers appraise facts, cheek touchers give evidence a longer, more scrutinizing look.

The Chin Push

The chin push is an indicator of strong opposition. It is accomplished by grabbing the chin intensely between the thumb and fingers, with the thumb pointing up and the fingers curling down and around the chin and then pushing upward. When a person cannot stand what is being said, he may grab his chin and push upwards as if to keep from screaming. This action locks the two jaws together and makes an outburst difficult, if not impossible.

The Chin Rest

A bored person typically engages in a sundry assortment of repetitive gestures. He clicks a pen, taps his foot or kicks his crossed leg. Few people will tell us we are boring them. Instead, they will engage in some redundant activity that gives them comfort, similar to that of a baby rocking in a cradle. In the courtroom, boredom can be seen in the careless chin rest gesture.

A person who doesn't bother to hide his boredom will rest his chin in the palm of his hand and let his eyes droop. Because this gesture is so obvious, the chin rester seems to be boldly signaling his irritation and disinterest. A quick change is called for if this happens in the courtroom.

The Eye Rub

When an individual places his finger over his closed eye and gently begins to rub, a negative reaction is revealed. It appears as if he may have something in that eye that he's trying to rub out. In actuality, that is seldom the case. Rubbing the eye in this manner occurs when the listener experiences some disharmony with what is being said. Children use this same gesture to rub the tears from their eyes when they are upset. Someone doing this in a courtroom may be secretly saying, "I don't see what you're saying; in fact, I don't believe it!" It is doubtful that he considers the argument being raised is truthful.

The Mouth Cover

We already know that when a witness is lying on the stand, he feels uneasy and possibly touches his nose. Under a tough cross-examination, with a quick tempo, a witness may also slip and cover his mouth in an obvious attempt to stop the false words from coming out. It is as though he is saying, "Oops, I shouldn't have said that." Typically a deceitful witness will perform the mouth cover in a more sneaky, subtle way. He will usually keep his hand partially over his mouth and talk through his fingers. In the courtroom, it is wise to be suspicious of testimony any time a witness feels he must speak through a hand. That hand is probably trying to screen a fictitious answer or distract the listener from what is being said.

The Neck Grab

Someone coming unglued by a demeaning attack, often will run his fingers through his hair and then grip the back of his neck. This response is one of the best signs of mounting frustration. It is as though the person is trying to keep the blood that is rising up his neck, from blowing the top of his head off. This gesture starts as a defensive beating movement. It is as if he were raising his arms to beat an attacker with open hands, then stops himself, by placing his palm on the back of his own neck. He is frustrated and angry and is giving the message that he feels the other person is a "pain in the neck." Firmly gripping the back of the neck makes a person look defensive, worn down and weary.

The Collar Pull

This gesture regularly occurs when a person feels he is in a pressure cooker or on a hot seat and feels "hot under the collar." It occurs as a person places his finger inside his collar, then pulls the collar out and away from his neck, as if to let the steam escape. When someone reacts in this way, he is getting heated up and is trying to defuse his own anger.

Scratching the Neck

In making an offer during courtroom negotiations, it has been said: "If the opposing counsel fingers his cheek, he is considering the offer from a position of power; if he strokes his chin, he feels on an even level in the offer; and if he scratches his neck, he is considering the settlement from a position of weakness." The neck scratcher feels uncertain about giving in. He feels vulnerable and is looking for reassurance that he is doing the right thing. He is nonverbally saying, "Well, I don't know if I should; it doesn't seem to be in my client's best interest."

The Arms

The crossed-arms posture is used throughout the world to communicate defensiveness. Avid football fans know that when the referee folds his arms he is signaling delay of game. Baseball umpires automatically fold their arms, and turn away when they anticipate an attack from a belligerent manager. Teenagers cross their arms in defiance of mandates or punishments handed down from their parents. In fact, all of us do it when we are digging in our heels to resist someone coming on with a threatening proposition.

Those who cross their arms during negotiations are thought to be rejecting, shy, unyielding and passive, while those with open-arm postures are judged to be warm and accepting. With this gesture, in particular, it is important to make certain that it is not a resting position for tired arms. To correctly interpret it as resistance, one should look for other defensive nonverbal signals.

Posture

Body posture and positions veniremen assume when being questioned, divulge how interested they are in what is being said and whether or not they like the attorney. Posture and position also indicate if possible jurors will be autocratic and whether they will be the leaders or the followers.

1. Watch as the jurors walk in. A submissive type will fumble for his chair to be convinced it will be there when he sits down—he is never certain of anything. A dominant leader, used to getting his way, will often sit down without even looking—he knows the chair will be where he wants it. He is used to getting his way.

2. Observe whether jurors flop in their chairs or sit rigid in an erect posture. Authoritarians will usually sit straight to show defense to the court, non-authoritarians will typically take limp body postures as they sit down.

3. Determine if jurors lean forward or backward as they are being questioned. The forward lean is a strong indicator of interest, a backward lean spells disinterest.

Body Language Checklist

The only safe way to operate as an effective body language reader is to cross-check each tentative conclusion derived from one clue with another sign. Even greater confirmation can be accomplished by using charts that reveal combinations of several gestures to reveal an emotion. Refer to the following checklist to increase your "reading" accuracy in diagnosing judges, witnesses, veniremen; in fact, everyone you meet.

Deceit	Frustration
Gaze aversion	Neck grab
Nose touch	Collar pull
Oblong smile	Skin pinch
Mouth cover	
Rising pitch	**Authoritarian**
Extensive hand shrug	Curved eyebrow lift
Increased hand-to-face movements	Tight lips
	Finger point
Fidgety	Rigid posture
High frequency of smiling	Beady eyes
	Steepling
	Answer "yes, sir!"

Skeptical disbeliever

Sharpshooter eyes

Raised eyebrows/
mouth open

Worry lines (parallel
bars)

Eye rub

Liking

Eyebrow flash

Full smile

Forward lean

Head nods

Openness of body

Dislike

Intense stare

Zero eye contact

Nose wrinkle

Compressed lips

Grapefruit smile

Closed hands

Finger point

Pupils constrict

Backward lean

Sympathetic extravagance

Big lips

Plump body

Casual dress

Dilated pupils

Wide eyes

Wears bright colors

Leadership

High status person

Crisp walk

Decisive sitting

Steepling

Crisp answers

Drop in pitch

Backward tilt of head

Rejecting what is said

Crossed arms

Chin rest

Nose bridge pinch

Chin push

Emotionality

Loud answer

Pupil dilation

Closed fists

Wide eyes

Compressed lips

Left-looker

Vocal pitch change

Darting eyes

Agreement with what is said

Genuine smile

Head nods

Head tilts

Forward lean

Open body posture

A PERSONAL NOTE . . . ALICE

I observed him in the halls of the courthouse. His stature was tall and stately and he had an extended air of confidence when he entered the courtroom. He held his head high and simply walked into the jury box taking seat number one. What amazed me was that he never even looked back to see if the chair behind him was positioned for seating or if it was even still there by the time he was instructed to sit in it.

His voice was strong as he answered each question with a crisp, authoritative, "Yes, sir." When he removed his glasses and placed them carefully in his immaculate suit pocket, his commanding body language led me quickly to believe that I was eyeing the jury foreman in this case. And, indeed I was.

ANSWERS TO EMOTIONS OF THE FACE:

1. (d)   4. (f)

2. (e)   5. (b)

3. (a)   6. (c)

Personality Typing and Birth Order: Everything You Never Wanted to Know about Yourself and Others, but Were Afraid to Ask

Happiness is as a butterfly, which, when pursued, is always beyond our grasp, but which, if you will sit down quietly, may alight upon you.

HUMAN DIFFERENCES

Each of us is different. There is not anyone, anywhere, exactly like you. Your uniqueness consists of self-concept and personality. How we perceive ourselves and how we feel about ourselves is our self-concept. How we relate to others, including all the different traits that influence our behavior, defines our personality. These are closely related concepts, because how we act towards others is greatly influenced by how we feel about ourselves. How we perceive ourselves is also determined, to a great extent, by how others act toward us and what we believe their opinion of us is.

Another might describe you as sincere, considerate, boastful, stubborn or shy. In fact, there are hundreds of additional traits and variations of each characteristic that could be used. Your individuality lies in the uniqueness of the combination and degree of behavioral traits that you possess.

As far back as 400 BC, Hippocrates philosophized about people "typing" and coined the distinct classifications as: Sanguine, Choleric, Melancholy and Phlegmatic. In the 1920's, noted psychologist, Carl Jung, developed the concept of "personality typing" to explain human differences. Today Jung's findings are expansively used for analysis in career counseling, management placement and marital compatibility. Companies use personality testing to gather information concerning organizational tendencies, leadership skills and communication styles in making their decisions concerning prospective employees.

According to Jung, each of us has two opposite attitudes or ways of looking at the world (extroversion or introversion), and four functions or preferred ways of gathering information and making decisions (feeling, judging, thinking, perceiving). The extrovert is described as a person who enjoys being with other people, is interested in the material world, and likes to be where the action is. In contrast, the introvert is a quieter person who enjoys being and working alone. The introvert is sometimes more imaginative than the extrovert and is likely to be more sensitive to nature and art. The well-adjusted introvert possesses a great degree of self-awareness and self-understanding. It is seldom, though, that a person is completely one or the other. In fact, a person who has a combination of introvert and extrovert characteristics, as most people do, is labeled as ambivert.

FACTS AND FEELINGS: BECOMING A "MULTILINGUAL" PEOPLE READER

One of the quickest ways to draw correct conclusions about an unfamiliar person is to stereotype that person under a general category of people with whom you are knowledgeable. Once you are sure to which group the person fits best, then the characteristics that are shaped by virtually all members of that group will be true for that person. Although when this technique is used in the courtroom, the attorney loses unique features of the individual's makeup, but an excess of valuable information in a short amount of time is gained. It is a method that is well suited to the voir dire examination, the time at which the attorney has only a brief interlude to make important judgments about people who will decide his case. What is lost in minute details is more than recovered in the expediency of determining accurate information about general habits of perception, attitude and beliefs of certain personality styles.

The success of personality typing depends upon a person's breadth and depth of experience with certain types of people and the speed and precision with which candidates can fit into a category. Trained observers learn to recognize quickly a distinctive behavior pattern or a demographic fact that is a predominant part of a stereotype, then the other traits that make up the common core of that group can be concluded. What might take hours or days to find out by individual questioning, can be learned in a fraction of the time by using personality typing.

One could talk about the Irish being warm, gregarious and sentimental, or women paying greater attention to detail then men, or white-collar workers being bolder and more daring than blue-collar workers, but these categories are too vague and general to be of great value in selecting a jury. In the courtroom, four personality types seem to emerge as having the greatest bearing on criminal defense and personal injury verdicts. The four personality types are: the energetic, the authoritarian, the perfectionist and the sympathetic indulger.

Categorizing people in these personality types is an oversimplification of a complex situation, but it can be a tremendous aid in counsel's search for a jury that is at the very least, impartial. Notwithstanding the overlap that sometimes occurs among the four types, it is still possible to improve the chances for a favorable verdict.

Before further describing the four personality types, let's have some fun. For ease in understanding the characteristics of the four personalities, they are being compared to commonly-known sociable animals in the following test. In the Animal Kingdom Personality Test, circle the letter in each of the questions that most closely applies to you. Once you have finished, you will get an idea of your own personality.

ANIMAL KINGDOM PERSONALITY TEST

1. When talking with others:

    A. I count words and think before I speak.

    B. I am straightforward and can be blunt.

    C. I am quiet and have to be drawn out.

    D. I am lively, friendly and open.

2. If I plan an activity, but get called to go out to a social gathering that I enjoy:

    A. I will not go out because the other activity was planned before.

    B. I go by the whim and I change my plans.

    C. I reshuffle my priorities and make time to go out.

    D. I agonize over which is more important, think of my responsibility and may go out or may not go.

3. I enjoy stories and jokes that:

    A. Have subtle humor.

    B. Are funny and get the whole group laughing.

    C. Are clever and have a witty edge.

    D. Have a plot to them.

4. I am best described as:

    A. Detailed and analytical.

    B. Laid back and nonchalant.

    C. Animated and talkative.

    D. Outspoken and open.

5.   When playing games such as cards, golf, etc.:

    A.   I look to improve my game and keep analyzing how it could be done.

    B.   Whoever wins is fine with me.

    C.   I thrive on competition.

    D.   I enjoy socializing and the game itself, more than winning.

6.   When I organize my work area:

    A.   It's about time because it's so scattered, it's confusing.

    B.   I'm doing so to save time later.

    C.   I'm a neat-nick and follow the motto, "There's a place for everything."

    D.   I rarely do; I believe anything goes as long as I can find what I'm looking for.

7.   I see myself as:

    A.   Confident and self-assured.

    B.   Energetic and vivacious.

    C.   Reserved and comforting.

    D.   Laid back and relaxed.

8.   When there is a cause, I:

    A.   Am basically non-committal.

    B.   Befriend the underdog.

    C.   Must firmly believe in it.

    D.   Weigh facts carefully before I give it my support.

9.   When asked for advice, I respond with:

    A.   Directness and openness.

    B.   Reluctance; I don't like to give advice and I typically step away.

    C.   Warmth, empathy and humor.

    D.   Helpfulness to the person in analyzing the facts.

10. When competing and I happen to lose:

    A.   I know that I will do better next time.

    B.   I wonder why I competed anyway.

    C.   I am disappointed, but I recover quickly.

    D.   I think, "Oh, well," and shrug it off.

11. When I do win, I am:

    A.   Content.

    B.   Proud.

    C.   Animatedly delighted.

    D.   Reserved about it.

12. When I work on a committee, I prefer:

    A.   To take charge and lead.

    B.   To help organize and handle details.

    C.   To be an observer and help; if I am asked.

    D.   To join in the fun and actively help.

13. The type of work that I prefer:

    A.   Is in the field of law, leadership or construction.

    B.   Is in the field of science, lab work or research.

    C.   Is social work, charity work, the clergy or entertainment.

    D.   Is in the field of counseling or veterinary medicine.

14. When planning a vacation:

    A.   I feel that my own back yard would be nice.

    B.   I plan one that keeps me moving and active.

    C.   I am fine with a book and the place I went last year.

    D.   I like experiencing new and exciting places.

15. When asked to settle a dispute:

    A.   I remain level headed and advise thoughtfully.

    B.   I am helpful, but know my limits.

    C.   I get embroiled in the problem.

    D.   I prefer to step away; it's none of my business.

16. As host/hostess you will find me:

  A. Resting, having carefully planned the evening, everyone is on his own.

  B. Setting the mood for fun and getting people to "let their hair down."

  C. With a small group of close friends.

  D. Involved in introducing new things and people to the group.

17. When I drive:

  A. I am not always consistent with speed.

  B. I think, "What's the rush, I'll get there."

  C. I obey the speed limit whenever possible.

  D. I have a heavy foot and like challenges on the road.

18. To me, graphoanalysis or any new subject is:

  A. Fun, if it does not get too heavy.

  B. Not interesting, as my interests are set.

  C. Interesting and it's something else to learn.

  D. Okay if it can personally help me.

19. When out in public, I:

  A. Dress primarily with comfort in mind.

  B. Dress for success and career.

  C. Dress with coordination and details as my main concern.

  D. Dress to fit my changeable moods.

20. The kinds of lectures and speeches I enjoy:

  A. Are casual and short.

  B. Are informative and educational.

  C. Are lively and filled with fun stories.

  D. Are persuasive and convey a message.

The Animal Kingdom Test is titled just so because it describes for us our personality in correlation to a common, specific animal. The traits that immediately come to mind when thinking of each animal, Butterfly-spontaneous, Elephant-strong, Frog-persistent, and Turtle-patient, are the same traits that are predominately found in the four basic personalities. Now, score your test.

1.	A.	Frog	6.	A.	Butterfly
	B.	Elephant		B.	Frog
	C.	Turtle		C.	Turtle
	D.	Butterfly		D.	Elephant
2.	A.	Frog	7.	A.	Elephant
	B.	Butterfly		B.	Butterfly
	C.	Elephant		C.	Turtle
	D.	Turtle		D.	Frog
3.	A.	Turtle	8.	A.	Turtle
	B.	Butterfly		B.	Butterfly
	C.	Elephant		C.	Elephant
	D.	Frog		D.	Frog
4.	A.	Frog	9.	A.	Elephant
	B.	Turtle		B.	Turtle
	C.	Butterfly		C.	Butterfly
	D.	Elephant		D.	Frog
5.	A.	Frog	10.	A.	Elephant
	B.	Turtle		B.	Frog
	C.	Elephant		C.	Butterfly
	D.	Butterfly		D.	Turtle

11. A. Turtle

    B. Elephant

    C. Butterfly

    D. Frog

12. A. Elephant

    B. Frog

    C. Turtle

    D. Butterfly

13. A. Elephant

    B. Frog

    C. Butterfly

    D. Turtle

14. A. Turtle

    B. Butterfly

    C. Frog

    D. Elephant

15. A. Frog

    B. Elephant

    C. Butterfly

    D. Turtle

16. A. Frog

    B. Elephant

    C. Turtle

    D. Butterfly

17. A. Butterfly

    B. Turtle

    C. Frog

    D. Elephant

18. A. Butterfly

    B. Turtle

    C. Frog

    D. Elephant

19. A. Turtle

    B. Elephant

    C. Frog

    D. Butterfly

20. A. Turtle

    B. Frog

    C. Butterfly

    D. Elephant

Count your circled answers and place the number under the corresponding animal.

Butterfly

(Sanguine)

_____

Elephant

(Choleric)

_____

Frog

(Melancholy)

_____

Turtle

(Phlegmatic)

_____

THE ENERGETIC BUTTERFLY

This spontaneous, emotional person sometimes arrives at independent and somewhat unpredictable decisions. Since he is popular, he may exert considerable influence over the other jurors because he is a combination of intelligent, prestigious, affluent and powerful. He values himself over every other living creature as evidenced by his frequent use of the pronoun "I" in normal conversation. The butterfly personality, otherwise known in psychology as the Sanguine, is optimistic and humorous and likes to be in the center of things.

The first tip-off to this type is expensive clothes, rings and other adornments. If you get the opportunity to view his handwriting, you'll see light, quick writing with lots of ornamentation and curls in it. Also, he loves to talk about himself and his accomplishments. He will often recite a grocery list of personal achievements, but when you ask him to reveal any personal deficiencies—he'll beat around the bush and cite none. This potentially one-man jury can pose a serious hazard to criminal defense and personal injury litigation.

THE AUTHORITARIAN ELEPHANT

The ambitious authoritarian person can be a handicap to a criminal defense case because of his wish to punish those who are dissimilar to him. Authoritarians are difficult to influence and they tend to take command of the jury, just as elephants learn to take command of the jungle. The core of the Choleric's personality includes moralistic condemnation, blame of others, suspicion, obedience and identification with strength. The primary motive behind most of the authoritarian's competitive behavior is his striving for power and elitism. He will be compliant and defiant to those above him and dominant, righteous and severe to those below him. He will immediately reject any defendant who looks disrespectful, rebellious and alien.

The extroverted elephant is courageous and a natural born leader. His heavy writing contains long *t*-stems. To recognize an authoritarian during voir dire, first, watch to see if he sits down with authority; without even looking back to make sure the chair is in place. Elephants expect things to be right where they want them; they do not have to look. Second, look for signs of excessive respect during questioning, such as answering, "Yes, sir" in a subservient manner. Behind compulsive obedience is usually an authoritarian waiting for his chance. Third, ask indirect questions to find out where his values lie. One such question is: "What do you feel is the single most important characteristic that a parent should have in raising good children?" An authoritarian might give "Discipline," or something similar as his answer, rather than the doting parent who answers, "Love."

THE PERFECTIONIST FROG

Perfectionists have a philosophy that all benefits in life should be earned by hard work and personal sacrifice, therefore, they can be an obstacle for the plaintiff in personal injury cases. This type of person drives himself hard toward impossible standards of excellence and has a high tolerance for pain and discomfort. Since he is tough on himself, he is tough on others. He does not want someone else to get a windfall award for free, without hard work. Moreover, the perfectionist tends to be critical of someone sustaining an accident; he wonders why the accident victim was not more careful. The frog believes that there is no such thing as bad luck. Through diligent effort, good judgment and persistence, this introverted perfectionist believes that each individual is responsible for himself.

To identify a perfectionist type of personality, look for an individual who is meticulous in dress, but not affluent. Whether costly attire or less expensive clothes are worn, his style of dress reveals his trait for extreme fussiness. It may show up in spit-shined shoes for men or in an excessively precise coiffure for women. This Melancholy personality is usually employed in an occupation that requires compulsion and special care for details with virtually no allowance for mistakes. Accounting contains its share of rigid, demanding people, so does computer programming. This unhurried, but persistent personality's writing is done with heavy pressure and contains short, low *t*-bar crosses.

A variety of indirect questions may be used in smoking out a perfectionist. A question such as "Do you use a budget in handling your money?" would give valuable information into his personality. A perfectionist uses an orderly system of handling money, such as budget envelopes and daily balances, and would give an answer stating that. The frog personality is dedicated to routine and schedules.

For a criminal defense case, it is wise to include a Melancholy personality on the jury because perfectionists tend to make the prosecution overprove its case before agreeing to convict. Perfectionists will have parallel worry lines down the center of their foreheads; these indicate the exacting, worrisome nature of one who must not err. A woman perfectionist is usually a better risk to obtain a hung jury than a man because she will take exceptional care to be right and flawless. Having such a person on a criminal defense jury acts as a safety valve in case all other efforts fail.

THE SYMPATHETIC INDULGING TURTLE

This calm, generous, patient, deliberate person is lenient and accepting and consequently, is desirable for both the plaintiff and usually the criminal defendant. He is programmed to give away big awards and wants no one in pain. The Phlegmatic turtle personality is a combination of warmth, empathy and a feeling that pleasure is the principle good. While he treats himself well, he also wishes enjoyment for others. This introverted person dresses casually, suggesting that he is comfortable with himself. He is tolerant of his own mistakes and allows for flaws in others. He would enjoy impersonating Santa Claus and giving an unfortunate person a lucky windfall. This sympathetic indulger, who writes with moderate pressure and makes short, low *t*-bar crossings, would be quite hesitant to vote for someone's punishment.

When attempting to recognize the emotional observer, watch for someone who is slightly overweight, has warm eyes and wears unpretentious clothing. Ask questions about pets to pick up a sympathetic tone or inquire about tipping habits. This type of personality usually is a hefty tipper because he feels he can easily identify with the haggard, tired waitress who is scurrying around the restaurant. The turtle personality's eminent compassion is crucial in a criminal or personal injury case.

Extroverts

Butterfly | Elephant

Introverts

Frog | Turtle

THE FAMILY ZOO: UNDERSTANDING BIRTH ORDER CHARACTERISTICS

A mother once said, "I sterilized a pacifier that fell on the floor for my first child, I rinsed it for my second. For my third, I wiped it on my jeans." Dynamic relationships existing between people, who are distinctly different and who all live in the same den, constitute a family. Understanding The Family Zoo, or you might prefer the more dignified term "family constellation," is still another means that can help analysts in determining character and personality traits of an individual. Picturing a desperate mother who has three or four little "munchkins" driving her crazy, it is easy to see why "zoo" comes to mind. Birth order doesn't explain everything about human behavior, nothing can, but it does give clues about why people *are* the way they *are*.

Birth order—whether someone is born first, second, or later in his family—has a powerful influence on the kind of person he will be, the kind of person he will marry, the type of occupation he chooses—even the kind of parent he typically becomes.

Try the following quiz to begin to understand birth order characteristics. Which list of personality traits fits you the best? You do not have to match every characteristic on the list, but choose the list that has the most items that relate fairly well to you and your lifestyle.

A.   perfectionist, reliable, conscientious, list maker, critical, serious, scholarly, caretaker

B.   mediator, independent, secretive, extremely loyal, a maverick, compassionate

C.   manipulative, charming, carefree, talkative, vivacious, rebellious, negotiator

If you picked list A, it is a good bet that you are the first born in the family. If you selected list B, chances are you are a middle child (second born of three children, or possibly third born of four). If you favored list C, it is likely you are the baby in the family.

FIRST BORN: FIRST COME, FIRST SERVED

First borns usually come in uptight packaging for two reasons: Mom and Dad. Brand-new parents tend to be overprotective, anxious, and tentative in one instant, then strict in discipline, demanding and always pushing and encouraging for a better performance, in the next instant. For first-time parents, everything about the first-born child is rather difficult and there is little doubt that the family overdoes things. First borns are "first come" and they are "first served" by eager parents who want to do the job of parenting better than anyone has ever done it before.

First borns are the achievers, the ones who are driven toward success and stardom in their given fields. Fifty-two percent of United States presidents were first borns (only four have been the babies in their families). Also, first borns are overrepresented among *Who's Who in America* and *American Men and Women of Science*, as well as among Rhodes scholars and university professors. They automatically fit into the category labeled "advanced." It is not their idea, but with only adults for models they naturally take on more adult characteristics. First-born children grow up to be conservative perfectionists who thrive on being in control and who are known for their exceptional powers of concentration. They have high expectations and a strong need to be the leader. They become the family standard-bearers and are conscientious in all their endeavors. First borns do not like to make mistakes; they are careful and calculating and are usually sticklers for rules and regulations.

On a jury, first borns are known for asking a lot of questions and wanting all the details. They are natural leaders who are able to size up the situation, outline what has to be done and then apply a logical step-by-step process to reach a solution.

FIRST BORN: THE LONELY ONLY

Only children—especially those who grew up in exceptionally disciplined and structured homes—are superreliable and superconscientious. What they say they will accomplish, they usually do. On the outside they are on top of things, articulate and mature. They appear to have it all together. Yet so often, they feel inferior and not "up to par." The reason for this is that their standards have always come from adults and have always been high—a little too high. Only children often feel "not quite good enough," and generally feel that they have never had a childhood. Even as children, so much was expected of them that they always feel as though they were adults.

The perfect description of the only child is to use all the words that apply to first borns: perfectionist, reliable, conscientious, critical, serious, scholarly, cautious and conservative, but precede each label with the word *super*. Only children are often labeled selfish and self-centered because they never had to learn to share with brothers and sisters and had no competition for attention from Mom and Dad. They tend to be "spoiled," but are often lonely and unpopular with their peers. Only children want things just so, and when things go otherwise, they may get irritable. In fact, they get very impatient with or intolerant of, people who don't measure up to their standards. Many only children can be interesting blends of the characteristics of oldest child and youngest child. They can act very much in charge and be very adept at handling adult situations, but inside they are scared, rebellious and angry. Because they have been so spoiled and pampered, they are not anywhere near as in control as they try to look. Because only children are "first borns in triplicate," look for them to be the superperfectionists who are exceedingly critical in work situations and in the jury box.

MIDDLE CHILD: THE GLUE THAT HOLDS THE FAMILY TOGETHER

Middle children (anyone born somewhere between the first born and the last born) were born *too* late to get the privileges and special treatment the first borns seem to inherit by right, and born *too* soon to strike the bonanza that many last borns enjoy.

Because later-born children "bounce off" the ones directly above them, there is no way to predict which way they might go, or how their personalities might develop. Any time a second-born child enters the family, his life style will be influenced by his older sibling. If he senses he can compete with the older sibling, he may do so. But, if the older brother or sister is stronger, smarter, etc., the second born typically shoots off in another direction. Any number of life styles can appear, but *they all play off the first born* sibling. The general conclusion of all research studies done on birth order is that the second borns will probably be somewhat the opposite of first borns.

The middle child is the product of many pressures coming from different directions. He experiences the "squeeze" from above and below and often indicates that he did not feel special growing up. The family photo album is a telltale sign that the middle child possibly got bypassed and upstaged by the younger or older siblings; typically there are hundreds of pictures of the first born in the album and only thirteen of the middle child.

Friends become direly important to the middle-born child. At home the first born and last born are special; with his friends, the middle born feels special. The middle child becomes a bit of a "free spirit," and is usually the first one to leave home. Lucky for them that they could not have Mom and Dad all to themselves and get their way, they learn to negotiate and compromise and become good mediators.

The middle-born child is the most secretive of all the birth orders. Since he was paid less attention to as a child, he plays it "closer to the vest" in his relationships and chooses not to confide in very many people. His "I'll show them" attitude goes back to the day his older sister got the chance to get new shoes and he didn't, so, a couple of hours later he got grounded for a month because he slugged his little brother for being such a pest; tends to stay with him throughout his lifetime.

Middle children are tenacious adults who are used to life being rather unfair. They are accepting in relationships and have remarkable empathy for people. They possess an insightful characteristic of compassion, which makes them excellent jurors for the plaintiff in personal injury cases. Middle children are successful managers and leaders because they understand compromise and negotiation.

FAMILY BABY: BORN LAST BUT SELDOM LEAST

If the first born is labeled the lion of the family, the last born can be called the "cub." Youngest children in the family are typically the outgoing charmers, the personable manipulators. Besides being affectionate, uncomplicated, carefree, vivacious and a bit absentminded, they can also be rebellious, critical, temperamental, spoiled, impatient and impulsive. Beneath that independent disguise, there is an inner rebel who gets away with murder. They can be abrupt and brash; they often go ahead and *do it* and worry about repercussions later. Last borns want to make their mark and show their older brothers and sisters, their parents and the world that they are a force to be reckoned with.

Last borns carry the curse of not being taken very seriously, first by their families and then by the world. Sometimes the older siblings laugh at the babies who still believe in fantasies like Santa Claus and the Tooth Fairy. Last-born children instinctively know and understand that their knowledge and ability carry far less weight than that of their older brothers and sisters. Usually their parents get all "taught out" by the time they are born and most of their instruction comes from their brothers and sisters. They are treated with ambivalence—cuddled and spoiled one minute, put down and made fun of the next, therefore, in self defense, they grow up with an independent cockiness that helps cover their self-doubt and confusion.

Last borns are suckers for praise and encouragement. A little pat on the head, a slap on the back and a "Go get 'em—we're counting on you" is enough to keep a last born going for hours, if not weeks. While last borns are usually people persons who enjoy jobs that require interaction with others, ironically they struggle with self-centeredness. They need to have fun, enjoy themselves, manipulate others and like being the center of attention. Since they grew up "getting away with murder," they tend to be lenient in a courtroom setting.

In the study of birth order, there are exceptions to every rule and many factors must be taken into consideration. For example, in a family of three or four children, if there is a twelve-year difference between the last two, the last child could quite possibly be considered a first born or only child.

In the case of twins, or any multiple births, it is a fact that the oldest child (even by only five minutes) would be considered the first born and usually develops the tendency to be the first to answer questions or make decisions.

Another fact that is important to consider is gender or adoption versus natural birth. The only girl in a family of brothers, who is the middle child, may receive more attention, hence there would be a slight difference in personality.

PROFILING THE FAMILY . . . THE JURY, THAT IS

Although each jury should be selected to fit the personality of the lawyer, the type of client involved, the theme of the case and the critical issues that will come up, balancing personalities is a tricky process. For example, a righteous authoritarian juror might be quite adverse toward a run-down, derelict defendant who is seen as disobedient and deserving of punishment, but might be substantially influenced by an older authoritarian lawyer, who may be viewed unconsciously as an authority figure.

Selecting a jury is done not only with the attorney's style in mind, but also with full awareness of the theme the attorney plans to present. The theme gives separate facts and events a common meaning and explanation that naturally favors one side. Since a verdict not only depends upon how well a theme explains all the facts, but also how palatable the explanation is to those who hear it, individuals must be selected for whom the theme has meaning and acceptability. Although brainwashing might have made sense for most of Patty Hearst's inconsistent behavior, it might have represented a repulsive submission to a despicable group. Had the case been tried before a jury of individuals who felt that in their lives they had surrendered their wills to others who controlled their fate, the verdict might have been different.

In most cases, individualizing the jury can be done efficiently and effectively with the help of forensic psychologists and jury consultants. The chances of selecting "twelve men fair and true" from the jury pool are drastically increased when juror personalities and birth order are considered.

A PERSONAL NOTE . . . ALICE

When I conduct my handwriting lectures on cruise ships, I typically choose a half-dozen couples at random and have a little fun with them. If I see something ominous through my handwriting analysis, I play it down.

Amanda and Paul, traveling with their parents, were engaged to be married shortly and happened to be one of the couples I had selected for handwriting analysis. Their future, they told me, depended on my input—not only for their lifetime commitment, but for a "dream" house they were preparing to build.

I immediately spotted something wrong. Amanda's writing was very large and covered the whole page and her *t*-bar crosses were high, way past her *t*'s and flying across the page. She was a romantic—a dreamer with castles floating in the clouds, a true person with a Butterfly personality. She had a tremendous amount of scattered energy and there were not enough hours in the day for her.

Paul's writing, on the other hand, was tiny, clear and to the point, which indicated to me that he was very focused, detail-oriented and meticulous; all traits of a person with a Turtle-type personality. Every *i*-dot was placed directly over the *i* and every *t*-bar cross was in the center of the *t*.

It was obvious that Amanda needed people and Paul needed his private space, even though he enjoyed being with close friends.

Should I indicate that they may not be compatible, or should I turn romantic and tell them never mind the differences—that opposites in most cases attract each other? They could be a good balance for each other. Amanda would bring excitement and spontaneity to Paul. Paul would keep Amanda well grounded and maintain the necessary stability for the relationship to succeed.

I took the side of the romanticist and told them that they were made for each other; to go for it and build their dream house together. After all, handwriting analysis is not the answer to all problems. It is merely another technique for assessing whether there are problems.

The months after the cruise flew by and I was very anxious as to how their love match turned out. I need not have been concerned. I received a letter (would you believe it was postmarked Sugar Notch, Pennsylvania?) from Amanda and Paul with a picture of their dream house. They looked extremely happy, and so did their newest addition, a baby girl they named Alice Stefanie Wilson—A.S.W. happen to also be my initials.

Promise to Tell the Truth, the Whole Truth and Nothing but the Truth: Intelligence and Deception

We must always have old memories and young hopes.

The Whole Truth

Examples of when each is used alone and when used together.

THE WHOLE TRUTH is the moral answer to such questions as, "Did you take a cookie after I told you not to?" Such an answer might be, "No, but I ate the cooking chocolate." One must always speak the whole truth when morality is at stake.

NOTHING BUT THE TRUTH is more useful on social occasions. For example, the question, "How do I look?", may be answered with, "To me, you're always beautiful." Even though the whole truth would require adding, "but that dress makes you look like a house."

THE TRUTH is the most complex concept of all. It means getting to the truth of the situation, rather than the crude literal surface truth. To answer the question, "Would you like to see some pictures of my grandchildren?" with the direct literal truth, "No! Anything but that!" would be cruel. But is that the real question? The real question, if one has any sensitivity to humanity, is "Would you be kind enough to let me share some of my sentiments and reassure me that they are important and worthwhile?" to which a decent person can only answer, "I'd love to."

THE TRUTH, THE WHOLE TRUTH, AND NOTHING BUT THE TRUTH, the uncompromising of the three, is used on such occasions as following a subpoena, when we take an oath to give required testimony, totally, to the best of our knowledge, about a particular situation.

NOTHING BUT THE TRUTH

"I could really feel my heart thumping when you asked me about stealing the money. I was trying to put it out of my head somehow, but I kept getting like flashbacks of me doing it. It was hard for me to talk about what happened with money handling, and all, because I knew if I slipped up and said the wrong thing, you might think I was guilty . . . which, of course, I am . . . not."

The person who said this confessed to stealing over $5,000 from his employer, over a period of six months.

RAISE YOUR RIGHT HAND

Raise your right hand and repeat after me: "I promise to tell the truth, the whole truth and nothing but the truth." Look at your right hand as you raised it. Is it straight or bent? Are your fingers spread widely apart or are they held tightly together. Typically those who do this in the courtroom with a hand completely straight and fingers wide apart are terribly frightened and will tell the whole truth. If the hand is straight and the fingers are held tightly together, the holder will tell the truth, but it will have to be skillfully extracted from him. Those people who usually bend their hands when taking this oath, are those who are likely to bend the truth.

How many of us have ever told a lie? We do it as often as we brush our teeth, yet until recently, lying received little attention from psychologists. Could we really get through life without it?

Bella DePaulo, Ph.D., a psychologist at the University of Virginia, affirms that the lie is a condition of life. In a study, DePaulo and her colleagues had 147 people between the ages of 18 and 71 keep a diary of all the false-hoods they told over the course of a week. Most people, she found, lie once or twice a day—almost as often as they snack from the refrigerator. Both men and women lie in approximately a fifth of their social exchanges lasting 10 or more minutes and over the course of a week, deceive about 30 percent of those whom they interact with one-on-one.

"College students lie to their mothers in one out of two conversations," reports DePaulo. Incidentally, when researchers refer to lying, they do not include the mindless pleasantries or polite equivocations we offer each other in passing, such as "I'm fine, thanks," or "No trouble at all." Even an "official" lie actually misleads and deliberately conveys a false impression. Thus, complimenting a friend's awful haircut or telling a creditor that the check is in the mail, both qualify.

Most of us receive conflicting messages about lying. Although we are socialized that it is always better to tell the truth, in reality, society often encourages and even rewards deception. Show up late for an early morning meeting at work and it is best not to admit that you overslept. If you tell the truth, you are scoffed at far more than if you lie and say you were stuck in traffic.

Dishonesty infiltrates romantic relationships. The lie in the number one spot for couples dating is: "I'll call you." Eighty-five percent of the couples interviewed in a study of college students reported that one or both partners had lied about past relationships or recent indiscretions. DePaulo finds that dating couples lie to each other in about a third of their interactions—perhaps even more than they deceive other people.

Psychologists believe that anyone under enough pressure, or given enough incentive, will lie and that frequent liars tend to be manipulative and shrewd, not to mention overly concerned with the impression they make on others. Further research reveals that extroverted, sociable people are slightly more likely to lie. Certain personality and physical traits—notably self-confidence and physical attractiveness—have been linked to an individual's skill at lying under pressure.

On the other hand, the people least likely to lie are those who score high on psychological scales of responsibility, dependability, and accountability. It is also found that individuals in the throes of depression seldom deceive others—or are deceived themselves.

THE LANGUAGE OF DECEPTION

When a living creature is exposed to some type of life threatening stimulus, it immediately responds to protect itself. The stimulus is evaluated on its basis to harm. The creature then decides whether he must fight off the threat or flee from it. If he senses that the threat is too menacing, he will opt for escape and evasion, instead of confrontation or counterattack. If he views the threat as insignificant for harm, he may even go on the aggressive and attempt to repel or counterattack.

A human's Autonomic Nervous System is responsible for maintenance of the body's equilibrium and functionings. It has the task of making the body physically stronger in accordance with a perceived threat to one's well being. The Autonomic Nervous System is responsible for regulating bodily functions like temperature, breathing, circulation of blood, and a host of complex chemical balances. When it is activated, the body is prepared to fight or flight.

We have all been placed in the position of experiencing fear. Whether as a result of coming in contact with a person carrying a gun, a near-miss automobile accident or dodging mortars and sniper fire in wartime, our "fight or flight mechanisms" are in full function when we feel fear. Humankind, still retaining a semblance of what our brains and nervous systems once were, respond involuntarily in our best interests of self preservation.

A probing, information gathering session is not a polite, social form of conversation between two persons who know each other. It is a time when analyzers and critical evaluators of words, sentences and paragraphs, scrutinize everything said by the interviewee. The necessity to hide guilty knowledge and manufacture information causes most individuals to quickly learn how to adapt themselves to attempt to "survive the interview," and not get caught lying. An untruthful person is aware of having performed certain actions and must effectively filter his speech concerning these areas. When placed in a position of fear, and being in the grasp of the fight or ‚flight mechanism, language, in particular syntax and semantics of grammatical constructions of verbally generated data, will change in accordance with the degree of fear being perceived.

THE UNTRUTHFUL PERSON'S "MINDSET"

The term "mindset" refers to what a person thinks and feels about the questioner's topic. A truthful person will know that he did not commit, participate in, or have any involvement in the relevant issue of an interrogation. An untruthful person will know that he does possess knowledge (which he must hide) of the questions he will be asked in the interview.

When a human being performs a conscious action which changes reality in some way, the following general factor applies: If the action is not something automatic, like brushing your teeth or tying your shoes, the person's cognitive thinking processes involve some degree of "rehearsal" and consideration of the probable results of the action before it is carried out. Although some violent criminal acts, such as assault and homicide are the result of impulsive actions, many are not. Numerous criminal offenders think, plan, scheme and mentally rehearse their crimes prior to putting them into action.

Someone who has committed a crime will have thought about a list of excuses that he can use if his name is brought up as a possible suspect. He will have formed various overlapping "schemes," or ideas about what could happen as a result of his crime, and its discovery. Accounting for all possible schemes a guilty person has to harbor, is a complicated process. Factors to be considered in analyzing of the untruthful person's mindset follow.

◆ How the lawbreaker's personality, intelligence level and family background fit his answers.

◆ How guilty he feels about the crime.

◆ How worried he is about getting caught.

◆ How worried he is about getting shamed, embarrassed, arrested or jailed.

◆ How guilty he will feel about lying, when he is forced to deny the crime or that he knows anything about how the crime occurred.

◆ How well he can successfully attempt to blank out or suppress his guilty actions from his long-term memory.

◆ How "smoothly" he can lie about what happened.

◆ How effectively he can rationalize away his guilty actions, perhaps even in thinking, "I needed the credit card and the guy I stole it from has more money than he needs, so he won't be hurt by the little amount that I charged on it."

◆ How he views the interviewer who asks him questions about the crime. Is the interviewer easy or hard to fool?

Based on a combination of these possible alternatives, the lawbreaker, during a face-to-face interview with an investigating officer will also consider how much of what he can allow himself to say. He might decide that it would be easier to just leave out information about what he knows really happened, instead of manufacturing information about things that did not happen. His rationale for thinking this way is that it might be easier and less anxiety provoking to tell the complete truth about some things.

It is almost impossible to accurately predict the way in which all of these various factors might impact the lawbreaker when he views his situation of trying to hide his guilty knowledge. What is known, and what can accurately be predicted is that the felon (or any sane, nonsociopathic criminal) will have some kind of Deception Apprehension Schema. Whether it is high, low or moderate, in the sane, some apprehension exists when telling an untruth. For a sociopath, though, it may be nonexistent.

During a probing interview, many inquiries and questions bear directly upon points of crucial information an untruthful person must deny, cover up or plead ignorance to. In this respect, the untruthful individual is faced with two choices.

1.   Either psychologically and verbally create and erect a *defense* against getting caught lying or;

2.   Go on the *offense* as an aggressor to combat the source of the threat: the interviewer and the questions.

Typically rational people prefer as little confrontation as possible. Instead of lying directly, most untruthful persons seek to escape the threat of anxiety produced by deception apprehension, first by attempting to convince themselves that they do not possess the damning guilty knowledge, and then attempting to convince a questioner of this. But, reality and biology cannot be cheated. When a person committed, participated in or received guilty knowledge of a significant nature pertaining to a crime, it is highly probable that some details were transferred into long-term memory. The untruthful interviewee must decide and respond to inquiries that he perceives as threats by either lying directly (fight) or by being verbally evasive (flight).

When faced with a formidable opponent which one judges as hard to beat, the most logical solution is not by fighting, but by fleeting, evading or eluding. It is much less emotionally demanding and anxiety provoking to take the route of least resistance: evasion and indirect deception, instead of direct denial lies and deceptions.

THE CHECK IS IN THE MAIL

Most liars can fool most people most of the time. Even children, once they reach the age of eight or nine can successfully deceive their parents. Three of the biggest lies told on a regular basis are:

1.   The check is in the mail.

2.   This won't hurt a bit.

3.   Have I ever lied to you?

To this should be added a fourth: "I don't remember." For years researchers have attempted to pin down and focus on human memory and how it functions and explore the capacities, limits and performance of human beings involved in memory related tasks. Questions such as: What part or parts of the brain are active in memory? Why is one person's memory of an event different from that of another? and, How accurate is anyone's memory in reconstructing what actually occurred at a specific incident?, continue to puzzle researchers.

Deception and an untruthful person's asserted "lack of memory" about actions, events, incidents or behaviors, often go hand in hand. Most interrogators have experienced a situation in which the interviewee can unhesitatingly ramble on about insignificant and irrelevant details, but upon approaching an area in which guilty knowledge might be lurking, he suddenly smashes into the old "lack of memory" roadblock.

STAGES OF INFORMATION PROCESSING AND MEMORY

With all forms of "learning," there are certain common factors that apply. First, an observer or experiencer obtains information from reality. The sense organs for sight, hearing, touch, taste and smell have been designed by nature to gather such information. Once the information is attended to, or perceived in some way, it is changed into a form suitable for processing as it moves from the gathering stage into the identification stage. This point in the memory process is referred to as "attending to stimuli." Some stimuli might be attended to and some not. Many factors, both in the environment and within the observer, along each stage of information processing, account for what bits and pieces of perceived data will or will not be attended to, identified or retained.

The mechanism in the brain responsible for identifying and storing data is human memory. Event factors such as exposure time, frequency, detail visibility and violence degree effect the accuracy and reliability of witness memories. Other factors are those which come from the witness: stress, expectations and perceptual activity. A person who actively performs or participates in an event is learning by experience and is likely to have more detailed memories than one who is only an observer.

CEREBRAL DOMINANCE IN INTELLIGENCE, PERCEPTION AND MEMORY

Intelligence is a highly complex, abstract "thing" for which there are no such definite characteristics as long or short, red or green, light or heavy. When intelligence is studied or measured, what actually is observed is intelligent behavior or intelligent performance, not intelligence *per se*.

If we think in terms of intelligent behavior, rather than intelligence, it is easier to identify and build a basis for defining the abstract concept. The basis of intelligent behavior must be some kind of knowledge and information, in its broadest sense, and this information may have been acquired formally or informally. Knowing this, it can be determined that the impact of intelligence upon intelligent behavior begins with MEMORY.

A factor related to remembering information is the application of previous learning to current situations. This is the ability to transfer or to generalize, and some individuals have much more capacity for transfer than others. Persons well-endowed with this ability are usually found to be significantly more intelligent than those who do not possess a high degree of ability in transferring or generalizing information.

Other elements of intelligence and intelligent behavior include speed in arriving at answers and solutions and problem-solving ability. To arrive at a solution, a person must identify the problem, analyze it, think of alternatives, apply previous knowledge, make a decision and offer a solution. The entire act involves integration—putting it all together with balance and efficiency. The aptitude to problem solve is referred to as mental or cognitive capabilities. Intelligence tests provide a method of measuring this mental capacity and differences in IQ scores are sometimes indicative of differences in brain structure and brain dominance, as well as differences that arise from exposure and experience.

Research on the difference between left-brain and right-brain functions has cast new light on mental processing and on the relationship between intelligence, perception and memory. The difference between left- and right-brain functions is qualified by the mental activities which are processed in each half of the brain. Even though each of us is constantly using both hemispheres of our brain, at certain times and under certain conditions one will be more dominant. Over time, though, patterns develop which reflect a preference for one side or for the other.

The left hemisphere is the control center for such intellectual functions as memory, language, logic, computation, classification, writing, analysis and convergent thinking. The right hemisphere is the control center for the mental functions involved in intuition, attitudes, emotions, visual and spatial relationships, rhythm, dance, physical coordination and activity, integration and divergent thinking. Left-brain thinking has been characterized as "spotlight" thinking and right-brain thinking as "floodlight" thinking. The left brain-dominant person can put the parts together into an organized whole; the right brain-dominant person instinctively sees the whole, then the parts. Whereas, the left-brain dominant person analyzes and computes information inside his head, the right-brain person is visually oriented; pictures, diagrams, etc., enhance his learning. Approximately 38% of American people are estimated to be right-brain dominant.

We live in a "left-brain" society, where schools are almost wholly oriented to the promotion and glorification of left-brain mental activity at the expense of the development of those activities which are right-brain functions. Highly creative and exceptionally intelligent people function with good balance between the two halves of their brain.

Following is a simple summary of some very complex information. Showing the principle of the general rule of brain activity. In actuality, though, it has been shown that there are small or minor areas in both hemispheres that are capable of carrying on the activities generally centered in the opposite half.

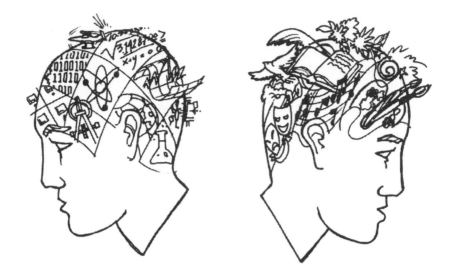

LEFT BRAIN, RIGHT BRAIN: WHO IS IN CHARGE HERE, ANYWAY?

Now that you have been introduced to the concept of right brain and left brain, you are probably curious about where you fit in. Following is a simple exercise to assist you in understanding your own style. If you are unsure of which answer to choose during the exercise, ask someone who knows you well to answer it for you.

Each of the statements might in some way relate to you, but in order to determine whether you are more right- or left-brain dominant, it is important to **CHOOSE ONLY ONE STATEMENT IN EACH SET**. There are no right or wrong answers.

1.   A.   I tend to concentrate on one task at a time.

     B.   I often juggle many tasks at the same time without any problem.

2.   A.   I prefer to think things through before sharing them with others.

     B.   I am spontaneous with my thoughts; words come out before I know it.

3. A. I prefer to spend leisure time with people.

   B. I prefer to spend leisure time with a hobby.

4. A. I am good at remembering names.

   B. I have trouble remembering names.

5. A. I typically do not read instructions before I assemble something.

   B. I typically read instructions before I assemble something.

6. A. I prefer being called "accurate."

   B. I prefer being called "creative."

7. A. I master a new dance or athletic activity by learning the sequence and repeating the steps mentally.

   B. I learn a new dance or athletic activity by imitating someone and getting the feel of the music or game.

8. When I want to remember directions, a name or a news item:

   A. I visualize the information in my mind.

   B. I write notes or underline what I have read.

9. A. In conversations, I express myself using exact, precise terms.

   B. In conversations, I have a tendency to make up words.

10. A. I can tell fairly accurately how much time has passed without looking at my watch.

    B. I have to look at my watch to find out what time it is.

11.   In school, I preferred:

    A.   Geometry

    B.   Algebra

12.   After listening to a song I enjoy:

    A.   I can recall a few of the lyrics.

    B.   I can hum several bars of the song.

13.   Sit in a relaxed position and clasp your hands comfortably in your lap. Which thumb is on top?

    A.   Left

    B.   Right

    C.   Parallel

Use the drawing of the brain below to record your answers by darkening the corresponding number. Remember, we all use *both* the right and the left brain throughout the day. What you may find in your responses is a pattern that indicates you are either right- or left-brain **dominant** in certain areas of interaction within your relationships. You may also have discovered that you are more or less balanced in your style.

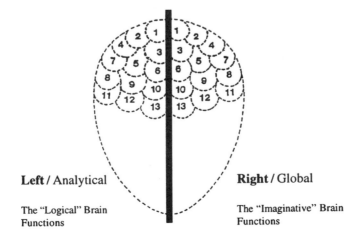

Left / Analytical

The "Logical" Brain
Functions

Right / Global

The "Imaginative" Brain
Functions

1. A. Left brain

   B. Right brain

2. A. Left brain

   B. Right brain

3. A. Right brain

   B. Left brain

4. A. Left brain

   B. Right brain

5. A. Right brain

   B. Left brain

6. A. Left brain

   B. Right brain

7. A. Left brain

   B. Right brain

8. A. Right brain

   B. Left brain

9. A. Left brain

   B. Right brain

10. A. Left brain

    B. Right brain

11. A. Right brain

    B. Left brain

12.   A.   Left brain

        B.   Right brain

13.   A.   Left brain

        B.   Right brain

        C.   Parallel (Darken half of number 13 on the left side and
               half of it on the right side.)

This analysis gives you a good indication of whether you employ balanced or predominantly left- or right-brain processing in your approach to the problems confronting you in your everyday life.

Such insight is significant. If, for example, the indication is that you are predominantly left-brain oriented, perhaps you are overlooking or neglecting the development of some creative or artistic talent which you may possess. If the indications are that you are predominantly right-brain oriented, then you are essentially a creative individual who tends to think holistically or in patterns and who may encounter difficulties in his predominantly left-brain-oriented society.

Right-brain thinkers, when confronted with questions of language, logic or mathematics—which are essentially left-brain problems—guess at the answer or may think in mental pictures or diagrams in an effort to solve them. They are applying right-brain processing to left-brain questions.

Carefully listening to the answers submitted by prospective jurors gives hints as to their preferred style of thinking. People who are to-the-point in their speech, are typically logical, left-brain dominant individuals. Those who rattle on are the emotional, intuitive right-brain dominant people. Typically, while listening in the court room, a juror who is left-brain oriented will sometimes look puzzled, thoughtful and skeptical. In evaluating and critiquing the message, he will rub his chin or brow and listen to all the facts before forming a conclusion. The right-brain oriented juror usually cares for the speaker and may look concerned or worried if someone is ignored. He likes to be involved in the conversation and tends to smile to encourage the speaker. He is easily bored with technical data and becomes fidgety as he makes a concentrated effort to listen and understand the facts.

In analyzing the jury pool, finding out the occupation of a possible juror can prove to be immensely beneficial to discovering whether he is right- or left-brain dominant. A representative occupation for a left-brain oriented individual is that of an: accountant, physician, engineer, financial analyst, banker, pilot, attorney, policy maker or computer programmer. A right-brain dominant person is more likely to be employed as a: social worker, nurse, entertainer, sales person, public speaker, teacher, homemaker, decorator, artist or actor.

Courtroom lectures, or speeches in society in general, require a fine balance between the left and right sides of the brain. Next time you attend a presentation, notice how it is structured. Are both right and left approaches included? Can you detect a pattern in the way the speaker moves from left-brain to right-brain applications?

If you find yourself following the lecture every step of the way, chances are that the speaker is shifting from side to side, alternating between precise, logical speech in a rapid, crisp style and some personal comment, a joke or a dramatic experience in an animated expressive style. Experienced speakers feel when the audience is with them and present facts quickly and clearly. They then release the tension with some right-brain gesturing, intonation and drama. An audience can remain spellbound for long periods if this alternating speech style is followed. However, if either style is sustained beyond four or five minutes, attention wanes or tension builds and finally the listener's concentration is broken.

To appeal to and hold the interest of the broad spectrum of listeners (right-brain dominant, left-brain dominant, Sanguine (Butterfly), Choleric (Elephant), Melancholy (Frog) or Phlegmatic (Turtle), a speaker must balance many elements. He needs to provide enough technical data to please the analytical person but not so much that expressive people are bored. He must show openness and comfort to allow for the amiable person's questions, yet move fast enough to satisfy the goal-oriented driver personality.

LIE CATCHING

Each side of the face is controlled by the opposite side of the brain. Take a photograph of a face and print one of the negatives backward, what you get is a mirror image of one side of that face. These two prints (the original print and the "backward" print), when cut in half and then reassembled, form two new faces. The right sides make up one face of the person, and the two left sides make up another face of the same person. Interesting images result.

The photo of the face made up of the two right sides (which represents a whole face under the control of the left brain) shows expressions that are keen, determined, hard and somewhat closed. The photo of the face made up on the two left sides (representing a face under total right-brain control) creates images where emotions are expressed more intensely; the smile is longer and higher on that side, the eye wrinkles are deeper and the nostril of the nose is flared more.

This exaggeration solidifies the fact that the right hemisphere of the brain has a greater involvement in both the processing of emotional information and in the production of demonstrative expression on the face. Seemingly, the right side of the face is the public side and that the left side of the face represents an individual's private side.

People relaying untruths will monitor and try to control their words and face—what they know others focus upon—more than their voice and body. Falsifying is easier with words than with facial expressions because words can be rehearsed, but facial expressions cannot. When emotion is aroused, muscles on the face begin to fire involuntarily. Initial facial expressions that begin when emotion is aroused are not deliberately chosen, unless they are false.

Extremely crooked expressions, in which the actions are exceedingly stronger on one side of the face than the other, are a clue that the feeling shown is not felt. Acute asymmetry of facial expressions occurs when the expression is a deliberate, voluntary pose; one made on demand. When an expression is involuntary, as in a spontaneous happy face, it is seen equally on both sides of the face.

Timing of facial expressions, as well as how long it takes one to appear and disappear is another deception clue. Expressions of long duration— certainly ten seconds or more—are likely to be false. Most facial expressions don't last that long. Unless someone is having a peak experience, at the height of ecstasy, in a roaring rage, or at the bottom of depression, genuine emotional expressions don't remain on the face for more than a few seconds. Even in extreme states, expressions rarely last long; instead, there are many shorter expressions. Exceptionally long expressions are usually mock expressions.

When someone is falsifying anger and says, "I'm fed up with your behavior," and the anger expression comes after the words, it is more likely to be false than if the anger expression occurs at the start, or even a moment before the words. Facial expressions that are not synchronized with words are likely to be deception clues. Emotions are hard to conceal. They make involuntary changes in a person's expression, his voice and breathing patterns and how he thinks. When micro expressions do not match the words spoken, the message is likely to be untruthful. It takes 1/25 of a second to observe a slipped gesture that determines a lie.

Not only is the timing of emotions important, so is the *type* of emotion or gesture. An obvious incongruence between emotion and speech usually indicates that the speaker is lying. One person may say to another, "Why are you angry?" The other fumes and answers, "I'm not mad!" The anger (emotion) is not in keeping with the words spoken and an untruth usually has been spoken. When an individual is hiding anger or sadness, he may try to smile bravely and relax his face. But, few of us can prevent our lips from narrowing when angry or our eyebrows from raising and eyes widening when we're afraid.

FIFTEEN WAYS TO LIE WITHOUT REALLY LYING

The following clues to deception can be used independently or in conjunction with one another. While some are excellent indictors by themselves, all clues should be viewed within the context of the situation at hand; they are not absolutes. Some of these are so subtle that they can easily be missed, others may be glaringly obvious. In some cases, there will be lies of omission—what is missing that should be there. Other times, there will be lies of commission—things said or done that are inconsistent with the rest of the message.

Once you realize that you are being lied to, should you confront the liar immediately? Usually not. The best approach is to note the fact in your mind and continue with the conversation, trying to extract more information. Once you confront someone who has lied to you, the tone of the conversation changes and gathering additional facts becomes difficult. Therefore, it is wise to wait until you have all the evidence you want and then decide whether to confront the person at that time or hold off to figure how you can best use the information to your advantage.

1.   **Unfinished Business:** An admission that there is more information concerning a certain topic or issue. Examples are phrases such as: "That's about it;" "That's about the size of it;" "That's about all;" "I guess that's about all."

2.   **"I Can't":** An admission that information to a question cannot be given; he could if he wanted to, but will not. Examples of this are phrases such as: "I can't say;" "I can't think of anything;" "I can't tell you anything about that; I can say this;" "I can only tell you."

3.   **Hypothetically Structured Phrase:** The speaker uses conditional verbs to preface his responses. Examples are words such as: could; would; should or ought. The person only says that he *could* give an answer, but in reality he does not give one.

4.   **Hard Question:** The interviewee is unintentionally using language to his advantage by telling the interviewer the complete truth about how he feels concerning the question. He states that he does not like the question, or that it is a hard question for him to answer or that he is having difficulty answering the question. While using these phrases, the interviewee is also stalling for time.

5.   **Objection:** This type of evasive response is uttered when a person has been asked a question about what he perceives to be a "sensitive" issue, similar to that of an attorney who stands up in court and yells, "Objection, your honor."

6.   **No Pause for Reflection**: When a question is asked which should require some memory search and the interviewee immediately responds with an "I don't know," or "I don't think so."

7.   **Maintenance of Dignity:** The interviewee indicates in some way that he is offended that he is being asked such a question. An example is: "I beg your pardon."

8.   **The Interrogatory Evasive Response:** This response is a question in response to a question. Examples are: "How should I know that?" "How would I know?"

9. **Projection:** This evasive response is a psychological defense mechanism in which a person actually voices his own fears while attributing those fears to someone else. An example is: "Someone would have to be sick to do something like that!"

10. **No Proof:** The interviewee declares that there is no proof which links him to the topic of the interview, or the specific topic of a question.

11. **The Answer Is:** When asked a series of questions, the interviewee prefaces one or more of his verbal responses with a form of, "The answer is...." while just answering "yes" or "no" to other questions.

12. **Rambling Dissertation:** The person's verbal response contains some of the information called for in the question, in addition to a lot of seemingly irrelevant verbal data.

13. **The Answer Does Not Equal the Question:** The interviewee's response does not equate to what was specifically called for in the topic of the question.

14. **Denial Of Presence:** The speaker implies that the question is being asked to someone else, although only he and the interviewer are conversing. Examples are: "Are you talking to me?" "Who me?" "Is that question directed to me?"

15. **Speech Errors:** The person exchanges, omits, adds or deletes words or parts of words which change the meaning of the answer, or make it illogical. The term "Freudian slip" arose as a result of Freud's analysis of slips of the tongue. He theorized that "slips" revealed a sort of "subconscious agenda" going on below the surface of one's conscious awareness.

IT WAS SOMETHING THAT HE SAID

Two salespeople can read all the manuals on selling and learn all the sales pitches that exist, and one will still sell far more than the other. While the two speak the same words, those words convey completely different messages. How something is said is often just as important as what is said.

Emphasis on different parts of a sentence can convey completely different meanings. Notice the different ways in which the phrase "Michelle was caught stealing from her boss," can be interpreted depending upon where the emphasis is placed.

Michelle / was / caught / stealing / from her / boss

a   b   c   d   e   f

a. By emphasizing the name *Michelle*, one conveys the significance of who did the stealing.

b. Emphasis on *was* draws attention to the fact that it has already happened.

c. Emphasis on *caught* indicates that the fact that she got caught is unusual.

d. Emphasis on *stealing* lets us know that stealing is out of character for her.

e. If *from her* is emphasized, the fact that she stole from her own boss is unusual.

f. Emphasis on *boss* shows that it was unusual for her to steal from a boss—any boss.

THE BLIND SPOT

Most lies succeed because no one goes through the work to figure out how to catch them. Lie checking is not a simple task, quickly done. Questions have to be considered to estimate whether or not mistakes are likely and, if they are, what king of mistakes to expect and how to spot those mistakes in particular behavioral clues. Questions have to be asked about the nature of the lie itself; about the characteristics of the specific liar and of the specific lie catcher. The hardest lies are those about emotion felt at the time of the lie; the stronger the emotions and the greater the number of different emotions that have to be concealed, the harder the lie will be to cover up.

Successful lie catchers find the missing pieces; they are continuously searching for the blind spot. The blind spot is an apt physiological metaphor for our failure to see things as they are in actuality. In physiology, the blind spot is the gap in our field of vision that results from the architecture of the eye.

It is enlightening to find one's blind spot in life. The deadening of one's pain through the warping of awareness is typically what is labeled as psychological blind spot. It's a way to filter out information that is often too painful to remember. Rejected information, like pain, lends itself to a distorted awareness of sense and therefore, causes stress in an individual. The threat of pain is the essence of stress: an animal fleeing a predator is aware of the danger long before it experiences pain, if it does at all. An individual hiding or suppressing information will try to keep others from knowing. In deciding whether a story is truthful or not, one must always be aware of his own blind spot and learn to listen and watch with both eyes open.

How Much Can We Keep in Mind: Known Limitations of Eyewitness Testimony

An experienced trial attorney knows when an eyewitness is giving deceptive testimony. A chill goes down his back as he listens to the witness distort, skew and exaggerate the event. The attorney has learned through courtroom experience that witnesses, in varying degrees, may exceed their natural limitations in recalling what took place. After a while, the attorney can instinctively sense it. It may be something about the way the woman speaks when she insists, "I'm positive the truck driver did not signal before he pulled out into traffic and hit the car." The attorney might know the witness misperceived, but knowing it and proving it are two different things.

The object of the remainder of this chapter is to provide a systematic technique of attacking eyewitness testimony in civil and criminal cases. In spite of the injustice that may result from heavy reliance on eyewitness testimony, it remains highly regarded in the courtroom as crucial evidence. For example, if a person remembers the train engineer blowing a whistle before the train struck the car at the railroad crossing, the railroad may be exonerated from blame. Discrediting of a witness may be completed by expert psychological testimony that explains to the jury how fear, distraction, memory rehearsal, expectancy, suggestibility and brevity of perception, effect and distort testimony. In light of the recent research on memory and perception, it may now be possible for lawyers to turn cases around by proving that a witness reported seeing or hearing more than is physically possible.

Perception is vast, but brief. It only lasts for about a quarter of a second; after that one relies on short-term memory, which has a reduced capacity for holding information. If a witness could be questioned within a quarter of a second after an incident has occurred, his account would be rich in detail and fairly complete. But, once a half a second has passed, he is dealing with his short-term memory that has an extremely limited capacity.

When information perceived is transferred into short-term storage, several problems occur. Since short-term memory has a significantly limited space, information is immediately lost in the transfer. Some disagreement exists concerning the exact number of items that can be held in short-term memory, but most scientists report its capacity to be from four to six unrelated items. The maximum number of stimuli, whether they be numbers, words, letters or marbles, that can be recalled from immediate memory is seven.

How many times do we begin to dial a seven-digit telephone number only to stop and have to look it up again? Typically, we are forced to pick and choose the most important information, the rest will be erased forever. Except in unusual cases where memory tricks are quickly employed before all of the details vanish, most of us are limited in our selection to about seven details.

Considering these findings, at what point is an eyewitness recalling more items than is humanly possible? In most cases, when a witness remembers seven details from a briefly observed scene, he is pushing his short-term memory to human limits. If he offers eight or nine separate pieces of information from short-term memory, he either has extraordinary powers or has exceeded the human boundaries of memory. Thus, one question an attorney must ask in his effort in discrediting testimony is "How much do you remember of the scene? Give us all the details that you recall." If an answer includes nine or 10 details, the hypothesis of bogus testimony can be strongly entertained.

A second problem arises once an individual has selected the limited items that are of interest to him, namely, he cannot take in any new information. His brain is tied up trying to hold the thoughts in short-term memory. Material in short-term memory must be rehearsed continually to avoid its slipping away before a lasting neurochemical change can occur. Review continues until the observer has repeated it so often that it is permanently etched on the nervous system in his long-term memory. Even then, without review, there will be some memory erosion over time.

The only way to freeze memory with rote memorization is to spend a monumental amount of time to overlearn the information. An example of such a phenomenon is in the learning of an Army serial number or a Social Security number. Most people can produce these digits when asked even though they may not have retrieved them in years.

In most cases, an individual cannot afford to tie up his mind on repetition because during this process his mind is not available to new, incoming information. For example, a witness trying to memorize what he observed would be unable to talk to bystanders, call the police or ambulance, or assist the victim. Therefore, a witness is likely to quickly code the new information for immediate transfer to long-term memory to free his brain for other activities.

How Witnesses Code Information

To try to remember details, we code information. Coding is when information in the short-term memory is pulled together, classified and filed under permanent categories already existing in a person's long-term memories. Sometimes the memory task is reduced to a single word. As soon as a person codes the information, it is in long-term storage and he no longer has to worry about it; it reduces the material to be learned from seven or eight items to one, and therefore frees his mind for other functions.

Unfortunately, while this method is more efficient, it is far less accurate than rote memorization. When a witness later tries to recall original details, he will go to a category and generate all the information subsumed under it. Details such as a facial scar and a tattoo, will have faded from his memory first and may not be there at all. Much of the time witnesses are probably delineating the details of a well-established general category rather than the exact features of their original observation.

Thus, another credibility question to ask a witness would be "What one word seems to bring back all the details of what happened?" If his answer is "heavy man," or "speeding driver," typically the shortcut of coding and categorizing, with all of its built in flaws and biases, was used.

How Witnesses Store Pictures, Scenes and Faces

Not all information is transferred from short-term memory to long-term memory by the techniques of rote memorization and verbal coding. Psychologist R. N. Haber insists that pictorial material is stored as whole pictures in the right brain and not as verbal labels in the left brain. Attorneys unwittingly will direct a witness to his left brain for answers that are contained in his right brain. When the attorney asks a witness to "Tell," which is a language command, the court what happened in the robbery or accident, the witness searches his language brain for the meager scraps of information he may have hurriedly stored under the axiom of robber or accident. From these bits and pieces, many eyewitnesses construct phony whole images. Accuracy of eyewitness reporting and identification could be greatly improved by directing the witness to the right brain with non-language suggestions, such as "Picture (image command) the scene you observed and then relate what you see."

The unbelievable accuracy with which a subject can recognize a scene that he has previously observed suggests that the pictorial image is stored intact in the brain. In criminal cases, a witness may be given a recognition test by having him look through a large number of photos in a mug book shortly after he has witnessed a crime. This procedure increases the odds of exactness and fairness. An observer is at his best in matching the raw picture stored in his right brain with an external source, while the image is fresh in his mind.

Errors in the Mind's Retrieval Process

Retrieval, the final stage in the memory process, also includes considerable potential for error. Similar to an artist who considers what should go here and what would look right there, the perceiver of an event must make decisions in later assembling the details of a memory. Unfortunately, as one rebuilds an old memory of an event, he tends to seriously transform it in three ways. First, the original scene is leveled in that several details are deleted to make the resulting memory simpler and more uniform. A long, craggy face may become smooth and egg-shaped over time, and minute details of a scene may be left out to make a more uniform whole picture.

Secondly, the recaller sharpens the highlights of the original experience, resulting in the salient features becoming emphasized and exaggerated.

Consequently, a two-inch scar becomes a four-inch scar and a .32 caliber pistol becomes a .367 magnum. The third distortion that occurs during remembering is assimilation, in which details are altered so as to conform to one's normal expectations, stereotypes, beliefs and habits of perception. For example, if someone observed two cars, a Corvette and a Volkswagen Rabbit going roughly the same speed, he may later estimate the speed of the Corvette to have been much greater, since Corvettes and velocity go together. Whether an individual's memories are verbal, visual or auditory, these memories are changed significantly when he attempts to retrieve them because of his expectations, stereotypes and beliefs.

EXTERNAL SOURCES OF ERRORS

Besides the cognitive defects that are at work during the recreation of a memory, there are factors external to the recaller that lead to memory inaccuracies. First, the retrieval environment can influence recall. Research shows that subjects are less correct in their recollections when they are asked to remember an event out of the context in which they made their original observation. This finding suggests that bringing a witness to the police station to identify a suspect or to simply remember an accident scene, reduces his effectiveness.

Second, once an observer has seen an event, anyone who questions him can influence the way he remembers what he saw. It has been found that eyewitnesses can and will identify people they have never seen and change their story according to the wording of the questions they are asked. In an experiment where 100 people, who had seen a short film segment depicting a multiple car accident, were asked, "Did you see *a* broken headlight?" instead of "Did you see *the* broken headlight?", different reports were received. Witnesses who received questions with "*the*" were much more likely to report having seen something that had not really appeared in the film, while only a small percent of the group who were asked the same question, but with the article "*a*," made the same error. Thus, even this subtle change in wording can alter the eyewitness account.

A third example of how situational circumstances act to skew the recall of a witness is in cross-racial identification, in which a member of one group attempts to recognize the face of someone from another race. Psychological studies clearly show that people are more accurate at recognizing the faces of persons belonging to their same race than they are at identifying those of a different ethnicity.

Under conditions of great stress, an individual's cerebral competencies decrease in several ways, all of which detract from his reliability as an observer. Because a witness may hysterically comment, "I'll never forget that face as long as I live," prosecutors claim that looking down the barrel of a gun improves a person's memory for faces. In reality, though, stress causes a person to narrow his attention, become disorganized and lose his powers of exactitude and differentiation. If a person is facing a switch-blade artist who is about to perform some unscheduled surgery, it is unlikely that he will notice his attacker's bushy eyebrows. Rather, his attention will be riveted on the long, thin, silver blade that is being thrust in his face.

It is readily seen, therefore, that there are internal cognitive factors and external situational circumstances that change the memory during retrieval. In putting the memory of an eyewitness to test, it is important to be cognizant that retrieval is not a xerographic process in which a copy of the original is simply made and provided. The original is faded and blurred and the gaps are filled in by the imagination of the witness. Believ-able eyewitness testimony, therefore, is a creative procedure of rebuilding the original event that has weathered and eroded by time.

During the final argument, applying these scientific findings of external and internal sources of errors, can help jurors exercise common sense to the circumstances in which the eyewitness functioned. Stating, "Now ladies and gentlemen of the jury, you and I know that no one can remem-ber 10 items that we're supposed to get at the grocery store," and "I ask you, how can a woman who was afraid for her life remember that the rob-ber had on a blue oxford-cloth shirt with a red emblem on the pocket?" By being aware of these scientific findings, jurors begin to view eyewitness testimony with skepticism and doubt.

A PERSONAL NOTE . . . ALICE

During a presentation in a Career Awareness Seminar, a young man asked if I could predict if he would be a good "cop." His body language led me to believe that he was rather smug and sarcastic and that he was "testing" me.

After studying his handwriting, I replied that I thought he would make an exceptional police officer because he could think like a criminal. His handwriting showed that he had the capacity to be several steps ahead of, and could outsmart any experienced lawbreaker. I also told him that I did hope he would use these tendencies in the right way and get a job on the positive side of the law.

The formation of his inverted *m*'s showed his insatiable curiosity and the breaks between his letters as he wrote his words, showed his innate abilities of intuition and perception.

The traits that might be seen in a criminal investigator's handwriting and that of a felon, check forger or con artist are extremely similar. Their lettering depicts an individual with a sharp, perceptive, curiosity, an elevated competence to pay attention to details and an ability to win people over. Both tend to also be somewhat manipulative, determined, intense and loyal to their own beliefs. There is a thin line between the positive and negative uses of such perceptive, discerning talents.

Appendix

— DO NOT MAIL THIS QUESTIONNAIRE —
CONFIDENTIAL — JUROR QUESTIONNAIRE

YOU ARE REQUIRED BY LAW TO COMPLETE AND SIGN THIS QUESTIONNAIRE AND TO BRING IT WITH YOU WHEN YOU REPORT FOR JUROR SERVICE. THE INFORMATION WHICH YOU PROVIDE WILL BE USED BY THE JUDGE AND LAWYERS DURING THE IMPANELLING OF A JURY EXCEPT FOR DISCLOSURES MADE DURING THE IMPANELLING OF A JURY OR UNLESS THE JUDGE ORDERS OTHERWISE, THIS INFORMATION WILL BE HELD CONFIDENTIAL IN ORDER THAT THE COMPLETED QUESTIONNAIRE MAY BE PHOTOCOPIED. TYPE OR PRINT CLEARLY IN BLACK INK. YOU MUST ANSWER EACH QUESTION EVEN IF THE APPROPRIATE ANSWER IS "NONE."

CONFIDENTIAL
— BRING THIS QUESTIONNAIRE WITH YOU WHEN YOU APPEAR FOR JUROR SERVICE —

EXEMPTIONS

All persons below the age of 18, the Governor, Lieutenant-Governor, Secretary of State, Attorney-General, Auditor of Public Accounts, Treasurer, State Superintendent of Education, members of the State Board of Education, members of the General Assembly during their terms of office, all judges of courts, all clerks of courts, sheriffs, coroners, practicing physicians, Christian Science Practitioners, Christian Science readers, postmasters, practicing attorneys, all officers of the United States, officiating ministers of the gospel, members of religious communities, dentists, mayors of cities, policemen, active members of the fire department, and all persons actively employed upon the editorial or mechanical staffs and departments of any newspapers of general circulation printed and published in this State, and members of the Illinois National Guard and Illinois Naval Reserve during their terms of service and for

Bibliography

Allenbaugh, Kay. *Chocolate for a Woman's Heart*. New York: Simon & Schuster, Inc., 1998.

Amend, Karen and Ruiz, Mary S. *Handwriting Analysis*. North Hollywood, CA: Newcastle Publishing Co., Inc., 1998.

Basic Traits of Graphoanalysis. Chicago, IL: International Graphoanalysis Society, 1968.

Bunker, M. N. *Handwriting Analysis*. Chicago, IL: Nelson-Hall Co., Publishers, 1966.

Covington, Margaret, Dr. "Jury Selection Techniques," *VOICE for the Defense*. Houston, TX, October, 1983.

Couric, Emily. *The Trial Lawyers*. New York: St. Martin's Press, 1988.

Cutter, Rebecca. *When Opposites Attract*. New York: The Pinguin Group, 1994.

Goleman, Daniel. *Vital Lines, Simple Truths*. New York: Simon & Schuster, Inc., 1985.

Gray, James. Jr. *The Winning Image*. New York: American Management Association, 1993.

Hargrave, Jan L. *Let Me See Your Body Talk*. Iowa: Kendall/Hunt Publishing Company, 1995.

Hayes, Reed. *Between The Lines*. Rochester, Vermont: Destiny Books, 1993.

Kuei, Chi An. *Face Reading*. New York: M. Evans and Company, Inc., 1994.

Leman, Kevin Dr. *The Birth Order Book*. New York: Dell Publishing Company, 1985.

Morris, Desmond. *BodyTalk*. New York: Crown Trade Paperbacks, 1994.

Munzert, Alfred W., Ph.D. *Test Your IQ*. New York: Prentice Hall, 1991.

Nelson, Nancy and Landry, Alice. "Oodles of Doodles," *New Woman*. New York: May, 1993.

Oster, Gerald D. and Gould, Patricia. *Using Drawings In Assessment and Therapy*. New York: Brunner/Mazel Publishers, 1987.

Richardson, Ronald W. Dr. and Richardson, Lois A. *Birth Order And You*. Canada: Self-Counsel Press, 1990.

Saks, Michael J. "Social Scientists Can't Rig Juries," *Psychology Today*. New York: January, 1976.

Samenow, Stanton E., Ph.D. *Inside The Criminal Mind*. New York: Ramdom House, Inc., 1984.

Sannito, Thomas, Ph.D. and McGovern, Peter J., J.D., Ed.D. *Courtroom Psychology For Trial Lawyers*. New York: Wiley Law Publications, 1985.

Springer, Sally P. and Deutsch, Georg. *Left Brain, Right Brain*. New York: W. H. Freeman and Company, 1989.

Thomas, Glyn V. and Silk, Angele M. J. *An Introduction To The Psychology of Children's Drawings*. New York: New York University Press, 1990.

Tickle, Naomi R. *It's All In The Face*. Mountain View, California: Daniels Publishing, 1995.

Wainwright, Gordon R. *Body Language*. England: Cox & Wyman Ltd., 1992.

Wonder, Jacquelyn and Donovan, Priscilla. *Whole Brain Thinking*. New York: Ballantine Books, 1984.